Greedy for Life

A Memoir on Aging with Gratitude

Chuck Crow, The Plain Dealer

Lori Stevic-Rust PHD

*This book is dedicated to the grandparents that
we carry in our hearts.
Thank you for making this world a better place to live.*

Praise For

Greedy for Life

"My culinary journey started with a love of people, family and particularly my sweet, sweet Nana Goodman! Even though she has passed, I am still comforted by her presence and wisdom anytime I step into the kitchen. I love the lessons that a grandmother teaches us in Greedy *for Life*."
-- **Jason Roberts, Celebrity Chef, Author, TV Personality**

"The theme of life lessons learned from our grandmothers is universal, and one that is uniquely captured in *Greedy for Life*. Dr. Lori Stevic-Rust's grace, wisdom and wit as a storyteller allows us to lovingly embrace our own aging process. This memoir underscores the fact that age is but a number. You will get excited about growing older! *Greedy for Life* is a book to be read across generations. It will make you laugh, cry, and hug people that you don't even like."
-- **Deborah Plummer, author of Racing Across the Lines: Changing Race Relations through Friendships, and They Still Call Me Sister**

"All of us pass through years, some of them tumultuous, which become milestones and force us to reflect to make sense out of our lives. Psychologist Dr. Lori Stevic-Rust experienced a year like that in 2012 and it has caused her to take stock. The result is her book, *Greedy for Life: Aging with Gratitude*. A self-starter who has always set ambitious goals, she nevertheless realizes that much of her strength and meaning come from the people in her life: her multigenerational family with it strong traditions, her beloved husband and children, her wide circle of friends, and the clients she helps. Her life's story has much humor, some hardship, moments of fear, and lots of joy. Its

conclusions are positive and reaffirming. *Greedy for Life: Aging with Gratitude*, is well worth the read."
  -- David Dix, Publisher Dix Communications

"As a columnist for CBC magazine, Dr. Lori had already impressed me with her writing talents. As I read Greedy for Life I realized more than ever how lucky we are to have her in our camp. While she describes her physical voice (inherited from her 100-year-old grandmother) as being "raspy and hoarse sound-ing" — not a bad thing, really — Dr. Lori's written voice is as crystal clear as it is sincere. And that's saying a lot. What an hon-est reflection of the author's life over 50 years. What a perfectly poignant gift for her twice-as-old grandmother, who no doubt already has everything else she needs (except for another World Series title for the Indians). Finally, what a great lesson for the reader seeking first-hand advice on how to age with grace — maybe even to 100 years."
  --Thomas Skernivitz, Editor Cleveland Business Connects (CBC) Magazine

"Lori Stevic-Rust's inspiring account of her grandmother's lessons of love and living encourages us to nurture our own rela-tionships across the generations and to hold them dear."
  --Pat Schraff, Schraff & King., LPA

Foreward

By the early 1990s, we had been doing two hours of live television every day for twenty years. There was no subject that we did not deal with on our program.

If, in our production meeting, someone mentioned an important life issue that they felt ought to be discussed, we would brainstorm over who should be invited on to deal with it. We were always looking for people who could help our viewers, and somehow we learned about Lori Stevic-Rust. After she had been on with us a time or two we all knew that we had found someone special. We learned that she was a person who could help viewers understand problems and challenges and how they might deal creatively with them in their lives.

How had this beautiful woman become so able at so young an age to address the complex problems of life? She was barely in her 30s when we got to know her, and for many years she helped us and the people who watched our program. She became our psychologist of choice; we knew that what she would say to our viewers would be helpful, comforting, insightful, creative, and important. We all felt it.

Greedy for Life is a wonderful and moving and often funny memoir that has given us some insight into how and why Dr. Lori was so important to our viewers. She was part of a big and complex family which held together no matter what problems came up. And we get to know about her very special relationship with her wonderful grandmother, sunny and funny and active as she approached her 100th birthday.

There could be no better setting for the development of the kind of person that Dr. Lori became. Humor, compassion, tradition, love, involvement, and understanding, were all a part of her upbringing. And those were the qualities she brought with her to the television studio when she would talk with our viewers.

Greedy for Life is an inspiring read.

Fred Griffith, Emmy Award Winning Broadcaster, Distinguished Journalist and Author

A Note from the Author

I am trying to imagine who you are– the reader of this book. Did the title pique your interest? Are you struggling with aging issues and thought this book may help guide you down that road? Or perhaps you were pulled in by the picture of the beautiful one- hundred-year old lady on the front page, who may remind you of somebody special in your life? Regardless of your interest or motivation in reading this book, I sincerely hope you will carry away at least one life message that resonated with you–that my grandmother's voice on aging with gratitude and humor was heard.

The writing of this little book was not an easy task. While I have written other books, they were academic, filled with clinical information, certainly not threatening and definitely not personal. During the writing process for this book, I struggled at times with my own sense of privacy both personally and as a psychologist. The idea of putting to print my most intimate life stories and then to share them with— well, with you, my reader made me feel incredibly vulnerable. But I was reminded by my grandmother that sharing our life stories is often what connects us to each other and inspires us all.

Our life stories in and of themselves are simply just that– interesting stories but the meaning of events and how we interpret them is what shapes our decisions and our life path. Almost every minute of the day, we are engaging in conversation with ourselves. It is through these conversations that we evaluate interactions with others and assess how we feel. But where does that internal voice come from? The answer seems to be that it is woven together from the myriad of voices of people in our lives, both past and present.

From generation to generation, we inherit our genes for diseases, our hair color, or our musical talents, but we also acquire our beliefs, ideas, and opinions. The power of these words and thoughts shapes the voice we hear in our own mind. These voices can be very powerful, and if positive and inspiring, can guide us through adversity and help us realize our greatest potential.

I am fortunate to have many incredible voices in my head. The encouraging and loving messages of my parents, the devoted and compassionate one of my husband, the playful and loving words from my sisters, the funny and kind hearted thoughts from my nieces and my great nephews, the supportive and challenging ones from my friends, and the little and grown voices of my daughters, who bring me pride and love beyond my deepest expectations. But the unique voice that is the loudest in my head is that of my grandmother.

So, in your hands is a compilation of some of my life stories, with the theme of my grandmother's voice guiding and shaping my thoughts and experiences. Over the years I have shared many of these stories about her with my friends, neighbors, family, colleagues, hair stylist, gynecologist, banker, and sometimes even strangers in the grocery store. I have come to realize that through the sharing of these stories she has become the voice for others as well. I hope you will embrace my grandmother's philosophy and you will become greedy for life.

Table of Contents

1 | *My Beginning and Her Near End*

"Nobody can go back and start a new beginning, but anyone can start today and make a new ending."

— MARIA ROBINSON

I looked at the clock for probably the fifteenth time already, and it was only 9:30 a.m. Traffic this morning was not that heavy, and I got to the office with time to spare; and yet I was already falling behind in the schedule. Where does the time go? I find myself frequently longing for more time. Time to complete what I need to do and often wishing for excess to do the things I really want to do.

What a strange phenomenon, time. It seems to be the one thing we all wish we had more of, but yet we are not always certain what to do with it when we have it. As a child and adolescent, time seemed to move so slowly. Those big events that I put on my calendar, such as homecoming, prom, graduation, and my birthdays, all seemed to take so long to arrive.

Now here I sit with time moving at warped speed, with events, chores, activities, and tasks zipping by me with more being added and never enough time to complete them all. Children growing, wrinkles developing, and what is happening to my hair…more grays. Need to make time for more hair color.

1

I packed up my briefcase with my unfinished tasks in the bag to be transported home with the fantasy that I may do some work when I returned home. But most likely I would end up transporting the same work back to the office tomorrow to add to the rotating to-do list. Feeling exhausted and overwhelmed, I returned home at 7:05 p.m. (yes, I looked at the clock again). I was greeted by my grandmother, who was sitting on the couch in the spot I had left her earlier that morning at about a quarter to seven.

Growing up, we called her Gram, but after the great-grandchildren were born, they started to call her Nana. The name stuck for all of us. Nana, or Emily Bernice Sitosky Serian, is a beautiful blue-eyed Polish woman. While her eyes are striking, it is her smile that draws you to her. The warmth of her thoughts radiates through her smile. When she laughs, her mouth is open wide without embarrassment as the sounds come from deep within. That same mouth can smile with pride, showing softness around the corners and with a gentle turning up of the lower lip her mouth reveals comfort and compassion during periods of sadness. Ironically, she is most self-conscious about her mouth, particularly the deformity of her upper lip. The scar she tries to hide with lipstick has been with her since her baptism day. Her godmother had pinned the collar of her blouse together with straight pins, apparently a common practice among women back then, and during the baptismal service, she picked Nana up and put her over her shoulder to comfort her. The straight pin went deep into Nana's upper lip, and without antibiotics, it became infected. The doctor cut the infected area away, leaving a missing piece in her upper lip.

Today Nana stands about five feet, even with her shoes. She has lost several inches over the years, thanks to her severe osteoporosis, which has left her with a significant arch to her upper back. At five foot three I feel very tall next to her. I brag about it. She reminds me that her excuse is osteoporosis, what is mine? But she *can* boast about her incredible skin. It is soft, light in color, even in tone, with only a few wrinkles near her mouth. Her eyes reveal the path of her years of laughing and smiling. She attributes the integrity of her skin to the years of buying expensive and exotic face moisturizers, which she still uses today. In fact, her one and only visible age spot seems out of place on her face. When she notices it in the mirror, it annoys her, but she begrudgingly admits that, "One ain't so bad for a one-hundred-year-old lady." That's right. Nana just turned one hundred years old.

While her face does not reveal her age, her hands do. Physically they are smaller, more fragile, with almost transparent skin revealing the blue lines of her veins. The joints in her hand have begun to curve under, creating a closed appearance. They look frail. But when I watch her use them, they are the same hands I remember from when I was a child. They reveal a lifetime of hard work. Below the paper-thin skin there are remnants of the strong and sturdy muscles that once worked the family farm. Her chores as a young girl on the farm were every bit as physical as those of her brothers, including milking cows and plowing the crops. Then of course there is my personal favorite childhood story she would tell about her responsibility for preparing the chicken for the family dinner. This lovely mealtime preparation began with her selecting the chicken from the coup, chasing it around in the yard, then "twirling" it until she could successfully snap its neck. This was followed by chopping off its head and pulling out the feathers before handing it off to her mother to cook. True story. We stopped letting Nana tell bedtime stories to the great-grandchildren.

Her hands not only worked the farm as a child, but also physically labored throughout all of her adult life. She worked long shifts in a Laundromat, in a diaper service company, in a factory, and cooked and cleaned in the family's own restaurant. At the age of eighty-five, she was still doing gardening work, canning tomatoes, and was even caught once pulling shingles off a roof. But the surface of her hands, the skin that touches you, is quiet and soothing. She still uses her hands in the most unique way that it is visibly noticeable by all who meet her. Whether she is applying moisturizer, cutting fruit, holding babies, or making noodles, her hands move with both surgical precision and gentle, oh so gentle deliberate care.

I did not inherit her beautiful blue eyes or her blonde hair, but I did get her voice. The voice can best be described as raspy and hoarse sounding. In fact, people will often ask if I have a cold when they hear me speak for the first time. Depending on who is asking, I may explain that it is my normal voice; it's actually my grandmother's voice, I may add with pride. Or I may admit to a cold that I don't have to spare the asker the embarrassment. My husband thinks it is sexy. Personally, I think it comes from the acid reflux disease that I also inherited from Grandma, but it's good that it sounds erotic to him. When I hear my voice after a television interview or on a recorder, I smile at the harsh, squeaky, rough sound. It's her voice. I not only sound like her but I am privileged to hear her voice in my head.

I put my briefcase down and stepped into the living room, where I snuggled up on the couch next to Nana and we began to talk about our day. I went on and on about the amount of work and how much I didn't complete, and then again asked the rhetorical question, "Where does time go?"

She smiled and said, "I was thinking the same thing." She added, "Every time I looked at the clock today, it seemed to move so slowly and the day seemed so long." Incredible. The cycle of life—time moves slowly, time moves too fast, and then it returns to moving slowly. Nana went on to talk about how difficult aging can be when you want to do more things then you are able to do, when you want to spend time on those things that make you feel productive and satisfied. I suddenly felt sad for her and a little ashamed of myself. I realized that I too will one day sit wishing that time would move quickly when I am no longer able to do the things that I love and the things that make me feel productive and valued. I'm reminded that time went on before me and will certainly go on after me…I am only afforded a sliver of that time. My sliver to date has been almost fifty years. Yep…I am about to turn fifty years old, and that is what all this musing about time and age is about.

More recently, I find myself taking time, making time, to reflect on how in the world I was to become fifty freaking years old soon. Even as I put it to print, I can't believe time has passed that quickly. I know that is what everybody says—well, mostly *old* people say it. You rarely hear a twenty-five-year-old saying, "Oh my, where has the time gone." I think that is because they know exactly where it has gone. They can account for the years, often with great detail.

Here it is almost fifty years for me and one hundred years for Grandma. If I am as fortunate as she to live a long life, I may be at my halfway point. What a thought. Perhaps fifty more years to live...what will I do with them? And if I have *less* than fifty years, what *should* I be doing with them? I guess this is what we mean when we talk about a midlife crisis. It's a turning point, a reality check, a time to pause and reflect on life. Will the things that I truly valued and wanted in the first half of my life be the same for the remainder of my life? I suspect they won't, and I think that is probably a healthy and expected thing, but the unknown of it seems a bit unsettling.

I feel a sense of urgency when I think about time moving and the things I still want to accomplish. I don't want to keep looking at the clock. I want to look at my reflection in my children, in my family, my friends, and my patients. I want to know that I have embraced my grandmother's philosophy, "Be greedy for life." She has spent her life absorbing moments like a sponge so they could sustain her later; giving, always giving, so she could feel good about what she was getting; and loving, not just the easy kind of loving, but genuinely loving people that I often thought were not worthy of her love. But it never stopped her. Carrying a grudge or a hurt seemed to be a waste of time...precious time for her.

Throughout her aging process (which for her I think started at the age of ninety when she moved out of her home in Akron, stopped driving, and moved in with my parents), she would often say she was not ready to die, but promised to let us know when she was getting ready.

"Lori," she said, "I always wanted to live long enough to see you graduate, and then I wanted to be here to see you get married, then to have babies. Then I thought I would be satisfied. But now I want to see my great-grandchildren graduate and get married and rock their babies. Time...there will never be enough. I will always want more, to see more, and to be part of more. I'm greedy for life."

I believe that she still feels that way, but I have recently noticed that some of her physical energy is fading, and with that some of her emotional energy and her greed for life have begun to fade as well. Our conversation on time continued a bit more,

5

and then our eyes met and she said, "I wonder what kind of time I have left."

Now, being a psychologist and relatively sensitive and an emotionally strong person, I handled this comment with all the grace I could muster. I responded, "You have as much time as I decide, old lady. *I* will tell you when it is OK for you to die." We both broke out laughing until we cried. She then added, "OK, then in the meantime, maybe we both should stop looking at the clock. Time is not always kind." I agreed.

My connection with my grandmother was born out of fate and destiny. I say this in a somewhat melodramatic fashion, but the story of how we met or almost didn't meet convinces me I am right in believing we were destined to share our time on earth.

The weatherman, Dick Goddard, was reporting on the extreme cold temperatures and the risk for significant snowfall. It was November 1962, one of the snowiest and coldest winters in Akron, Ohio. The ringing of the phone in the kitchen woke my mother from a sound sleep. The clock on the nightstand next to her bed read 2:45 a.m. While she was in the process of jumping out of bed, my father was already in the kitchen answering the phone. He returned to the bedroom and said, "It was the hospital. Your mother has started to bleed internally and they are preparing her for surgery." My mother recalls a feeling of numbness climbing over her and her voice repeating, "Oh my God. They said she wasn't strong enough yet for surgery."

Two weeks prior it was discovered that my grandmother had bleeding ulcers in her stomach. She apparently had been showing signs of bleeding, but she ignored them, believing that would heal on their own. One morning when she was on her way to work at the local diaper store at 4:30 a.m., she collapsed near the car. She had been hospitalized for two weeks while the doctors tried to stabilize her. They knew she had lost a significant amount of blood and was not strong enough for them to attempt to surgically intervene. Unfortunately, the bleeding had restarted and emergency surgery was necessary. My grandmother's recollection of that evening was waking feeling weak and ringing for the nurse; then she began to see pigs on the walls, and everything went black.

My parents arrived at the hospital as my grandmother was being rushed down the hallway on a gurney with several doctors and nurses running behind. One of the doctors stopped to tell them that she did not have a pulse and admitted that things did not look good. They saw that my grandmother was Catholic and suggested that now may be the time for the family to contact a priest. They went on to say that they had called a Dr. Fox, who was one of the best surgeons on their staff, and he was prepping for the surgery.

My parents joined my grandfather in the waiting room for what would be an all-night vigil that lasted until about noon. As family stories go, I am told that as the vigil of waiting for news of the surgery continued, the doors at the end of the hall finally opened. My mother recalls the hospital hallway being long and dimly lit, so when the doors opened, it created an image of a small silhouette of a man in a surgical cap walking toward them.

They all stood as he approached, anxiously searching his face for clues on what he was about to say. Dr. Fox, or as the family has referred to him over the past fifty years, "the man with kind eyes and God's hands," let them know that Nana was still alive but not out of danger. They had to remove three fourths of her stomach. He then gestured to my mother's belly and instructed her to go home and get some rest, as she was nine months pregnant with me. He felt she should go home to prevent early labor as I was to be born two weeks later. As my mother cried, he assured her that he would sit with my grandmother through the night but it was now out of his hands and in God's.

Whether God played a role in my grandmother's recovery can be debated by many. For her, she believes that her purpose on earth had not been completed. At the age of fifty, my age, she felt she still had so much to accomplish and so much to see and enjoy with her family. She always seemed to understand and accept that she had a purpose for being alive. With age that purpose seemed to become clearer and the drive to fulfill it became more intense.

For me, I wonder what my life would have been like if she had died and I had never met her. When I track back in time, decisions that I made, beliefs that I hold, and values that I cherish, I wonder if I would have come to different conclusions without her voice in my head. I sit here today incredibly grateful that on that early morning in November 1962, somebody intervened and gave me the ultimate gift of my grandmother. I received the gift of time, time with her for the past fifty years.

2 | The Best Gifts Comes from Flops

"Success consists of going from failure to failure without loss of enthusiasm."

— WINSTON CHURCHILL

O ne day when my daughter Katie was a little girl, she asked my grandmother why her arms flopped. She gently grabbed the skin under my grandmother's arm and said, "If you push this, it flops." She went on to ask, "Why doesn't mine do that?" Why indeed. These "flops" can best be described as the area on a woman's arm that appears to be a bicep that became deflated like a balloon and fell to the underneath side of the arm. As the wind blows, so do the "flops." Nana swears at times she even feels them slapping against her ribs. This motivates her all the more to continue to lift weights, as she is convinced that she can tighten up those flops. Each of us women who share her genetic makeup quietly sits on the couch and cheers her on in the hopes that our fate of the flops can be altered.

"Flops" are another surprising gift of aging. Or maybe to some degree or another, we all have them throughout our life, but only as we age do we recognize them as hidden gifts.

There is no question that life is easier to view in the rearview mirror with the passage of time. We can more clearly see how things that seemed painful and disappointing in the moment may have led to incredible blessings further down our life path. How the loss of a job may have led to a great career opportunity, or running late in the morning may have saved us from a deadly accident on the freeway. Some of our greatest experiences of flops, disappointments, and pain when examined closely usually turn out to be life changing.

One of my great flops had to do with a pot roast. I started to date my high school sweetheart the end of my sophomore year of high school through my second year of college. He was, probably still is, a great guy. Unlike many of my friend's boyfriends, he was thoughtful and kind. We had fun together and seemed to be compatible. Throughout the years he spent much time with my family, who also had great affection for him. He was just a nice guy — until the night of the pot roast.

We had been dating for so long through our very young years; it will surprise nobody to learn that we had developed into a nice comfortable friendship. The strain of me being away at college, and the budding interest for both of us to explore other relationships, had forced our hand into "talking about us." At the tender age of only twenty, we both seemed scared to let go of each other, but eager to know if there was something else to a relationship. For months we had danced around the topic, always careful to not hurt each other, but increasingly becoming more restless.

It was the first week of June. I remember because finals were finally over, and I was just completing a few things on campus and preparing to come home for a couple weeks before summer classes started. We decided that on Friday night, he would drive down to my apartment, and I would make dinner so we could talk about "us." I put the pot roast in the oven at around three o'clock to have it ready for a six o'clock dinner. At five o'clock, I made a salad and set the table.

The smell of the onions and carrots slowly roasting in the garlic sauce made its way downstairs to Nana's living room. She commented on how good it smelled and then asked how I had prepared the meat. She knew all about the dinner and what my boyfriend and I were to discuss. She liked him very much, but always remained clear in her message that we both deserved to be honest with each other, and what was meant to be would be revealed. I could not possibly know how true her words would turn out to be.

The clock in my living room chimed 6:30 p.m. I turned the oven on low to prevent the pot roast from drying out. I was beginning to get worried. I called his house, and his mother told me he was running late from work, but he should be there soon. I hung up annoyed. He knew how important this dinner was for our relationship. Why had he not planned his time better?

When eight o'clock rolled around, the oven had been turned off already for several hours. The third phone call to his home was placed and there was no answer again. I was incredibly worried. Something must have happened to him. On the fourth call to his home, his mother answered and began to tell me a story about how she wasn't sure, but she thought he may have forgotten about the dinner and went out with some friends, but she was sure he would call me when he got back. Now, worry turned to rage. How could he do this to me after all these years together? Did I matter so little to him?

By ten thirty there was no call from him, just more apparent lies from his mother. At about eleven I went downstairs crying, carrying my pot roast, and told my grandmother I was going to his house to find out what was really going on. She tried her best to convince me to stay until morning, not to make the hour drive while I was so upset and at the late hour, but she could not change my mind. As she stood in the doorway and watched me get into my car, she yelled out the door "What are you going to do with that pot roast?"

I called back, "I am going to give it to him." Nana tells me today that after she shut the door, she smiled and told my grandfather, "I wouldn't want to be him."

I pulled into the driveway of his house. His car was not there, so I decided to sit and wait. At 1:30 a.m. he pulled into the driveway, I'm not sure what excuse he offered me. What I do remember is getting out of the car, telling him that dinner was ready. I dumped the pot roast with the carrots, potatoes, and onions on his head. I got back into the car and went to my parents.

The next day I cried, felt sick, and refused to take his calls. This was the worst thing that I could have ever imagined happening to me. A relationship with somebody that I had cared about for four years was over. He hurt me, and now what if I never found somebody as great as he was. Nothing that anybody could say made me feel better. So for the next twenty-four hours, I cried and felt sick.

It should be noted here that I am not a pretty crier. Actually, I can become quite deformed in my appearance when I cry. The eyes puff up, out, and sideways, leaving me looking as if somebody took a baseball bat to my face. Then for good measure my skin develops red blotches, making it appear that I have been burned on top of the beating. Knowing I could not be seen in public with this face, I went to my sister Diane's house to spend time with my little niece, Jennifer, who was only two and surely could not judge my appearance. I spent the day swimming and crying. By the end of the evening, my disheveled chlorinated hair matched my disfigured face. The recollection of my appearance makes me realize that Grandma's arm flops were sexy by comparison. I felt like a flop.

I was lying on the brown sofa in Diane's living room, facing away from the front door and watching television, when there was a knock on the door. I didn't get up because I didn't care who was there. I heard the familiar voices of my sister's friends Doug and Debbie. They were introducing Diane to Doug's brother, Jay, who had been out water skiing with a friend all day and stopped over to see them. Oh shit, like I felt like making small talk. I sat up to greet Doug and Debbie, fully aware of how I looked but not caring what they thought. But as I sat up, my eyes went to the tall, muscular, incredibly handsome guy standing next to Debbie. He was in a pair of shorts, a tight-fitting T-shirt with biceps upon biceps that were the antithesis of flops. He wore a baseball cap and an incredibly warm smile.

Suddenly I wanted the floor to open up and swallow me. First, why did I care how I looked to this guy? What was that nervous feeling inside all about? For God's sake I was in mourning. As all of these thoughts were racing through my head, I heard Diane introducing me. I was doing my best not to make eye contact. How could I let him look at these eyes? I excused myself and went to the bathroom. I frantically started to put cold compresses on my eyes, knowing that in about forty-eight hours the swelling would go down—but how could I justify staying in this bathroom for two days? Instead I found some mascara that I dabbed on the ends of the lashes that had not been fully swallowed up by the puffy swelling. I grabbed a smelly baseball cap from the hamper to cover the disaster of a hairdo I was sporting.

I took a deep breath and re-entered the living room in time to hear Diane sharing my pot roast story. Nice ice breaker, I thought. Jay and I chatted for a little while and he invited me out to see his truck in the driveway. He had a truck that had been custom designed and had won numerous awards. I don't recall what we talked about in that driveway but I knew something was happening to me and it scared me.

Jay called me the next day to see if I was interested in going to dinner. What! Where is this guy's judgment? Did he not see my eyes and hear the pot roast story? Deep down I was flattered and of course interested, but not sure I was ready. After all, I had just dumped pot roast on my boyfriend of four years less than twenty-four hours ago. Was I ready to start a new relationship? I made an excuse about needing to get ready to return to school. It was true; I was going back to my apartment to begin summer classes.

Over the course of the next several weeks, Jay called a few more times, trying to make arrangements for a date. I made excuses. Finally, Jay asked, "What are you doing six weeks from now? If you tell me you are busy, I know you are not interested, but I hope you are at least open to having dinner at least once with me." I agreed and with anticipation put the date on my wall calendar.

In the meantime my old boyfriend sent flowers to me, to my mother, to my grandmother. I received apology letters and calls, and then one day he came to see me to talk about what had happened and apologized. He wanted us to get back together. It seems so striking to me today that I can still recall how I felt that day. I cared about this boyfriend who had been my friend and companion for so many years, but I never felt like I did thinking about that dinner date I was to have in six weeks. My path in life had taken a turn, a turn I tried to avoid and control. I thought what I wanted was to remain in a relationship that was familiar and comfortable. But fate seemed to know better.

I married Jay a year and a half after our first date. The award-winning truck that he took such great pride in showing me that day in the driveway at my sister's was sold six months after we met. It now resides on my left hand as a beautiful diamond ring. Jay and I will soon be celebrating twenty-eight years of marriage, and although he proclaims to love everything I cook, secretly I think he hates when I make pot roast.

Shortly after we were married, we set out the plan on when we would have children. We both agreed it made sense for me to finish my doctoral degree, and I did. We then wanted to wait until we were settled into a new home. So my father drew up the house plans; we served as our own general building contractor, and we built our first beautiful home. We moved in ten months later and began to think about children.

On a late February morning, Jay and I sat at our kitchen table looking through the bay window at the snow-covered lawn. We sat in our robes, sipping coffee and talking about how fortunate we were with our new home and our successful careers. We decided it was time for us to have children. We both always wanted kids, but we were waiting for the right time. This was it. I recall the feeling of excitement knowing that we were going to have a baby. Reading this, you may think that means I was pregnant, but it simply meant we had *decided* to have a baby. Isn't that how it works?

The first month I got my period, I was disappointed and surprised. The second month distress settled in, but when the third month turned into thirty-six months of periods, the despair and anxiety became overwhelming. How could this be? Would I never be a mother? The sadness every month had become unbearable.

The picture on the wall was of an iris flower. The colors were soft and soothing to the eye. I tried to keep my focus on it, but through the hour that we had been waiting, I found my attention being drawn to the big glass window that separated the fertility clinic from the waiting area where all the pregnant women were sitting. They always looked so beautiful to me. My eye caught one young woman who was gently caressing her belly in a rhythmic fashion as her partner had his hand resting on hers. They looked so happy. I knew they would be entering a room to hear the sound of their baby's heartbeat or would be seeing an ultrasound image of their baby. What a stark comparison to the room I was to enter.

The room was small, and the air often felt stuffy and heavy. I put my feet into the stirrups and waited for the doctor to enter the room. I tried to keep my thoughts positive. I tried so hard to squeeze out the image of the happy couple in the waiting room. The soft knock on the door snapped me out of the thought. I was about to have my ninth in vitro fertilization procedure. I knew Jay had already spent time in his room leaving a sperm specimen and now was probably sitting in the waiting room looking at that same iris picture on the wall.

The first few months we laughed and accepted every joke that our well-meaning friends and family made about the concept of Jay having to spend time with the donation jar and the "magazines". But today the strain of the past three years was weighing heavy on both of us. Our sense of humor was gone, along with our energy. For the past year and a half, I had been taking fertility drugs daily. A neighbor who was a nurse came to give me injections twice a week. Jay and I would have to plan sex, plan appointments, and then deal with the great disappointment every month knowing we would have to start all over again. We both had decided this was the last procedure we could put ourselves through.

Although feeling incredibly exhausted, we tried to maintain some sense of optimism that this one would work. On the ride home, we tried to encourage each other but it was clear that neither one of us believed our own words. The words *disappointment* and *failure* continued to ring through my head. When we got home, we both cried and decided that maybe all we needed was each other. We made love. I felt a tremendous sense of relief with the decision to stop the drugs, stop the procedures, and stop the daily temperature taking and the record keeping and the planned sex. It was over.

Several weeks later when I began to spot, signaling that my period was about to begin, I didn't feel the same level of disappointment and sadness. This time it was expected. Jay and I would enjoy our lives together — just the two of us. Several days later the spotty bleeding stopped without my period starting. I refused to allow myself to think *maybe*. Then another week passed without a period.

Jay and I stood in the aisle at the CVS store staring at all the pregnancy test kits. Some had plus and minus signs, some had pink color-changing indicators, and others used horizontal lines as a symbol that a test was positive. We bought one of each. I urinated on all three test strips and went downstairs to set the timer in the kitchen for five minutes. After the longest five minutes of our lives, the timer went off. Jay and I looked at each other and then without a word began to race each other up the stairs to look at the strips. Pushing and shoving each other through the bathroom door, we saw the test kits on the bathroom counter. A pink color, a plus sign, and the horizontal lines all were clearly present. We were going to have our first baby.

We now sat in the waiting room anticipating our appointments when we got to hear our baby's heartbeat and see her on the ultrasound. I had a few difficulties with the pregnancy, including the development of a bleeding ulcer, which led to a hospitalization for treatment. As a result I was having a few extra ultrasounds, which I didn't mind. I loved seeing my little girl move around.

Our name was called, and we walked past the fertility clinic windows on our way to the ultrasound room. I couldn't help but feel sad as I looked into the window and saw the pain and stress in the eyes of those sitting and waiting for their procedures, not knowing if they would be successful. I prayed that one day they would know the total joy we were feeling. We entered the ultrasound room like we had on many occasions. They warmed the lubricating gel and squeezed it on my belly. The technician quickly got to work, and soon our sweet little girl appeared on the screen. She was sucking her thumb and kicking her legs. What an incredible feeling. How lucky and blessed we felt. Our regular gynecologist had asked us to see a specialist to monitor the pregnancy, just to be on the safe side. We didn't mind. We were having a baby.

I was still lying on the ultrasound table and Jay was seated to my left when Dr. J entered the room. She quickly took the wand and began to move it around on my stomach. She began to speak quickly, using every medical term she could think of to describe what she was seeing in the brain of our baby. She began to use phrases like, "hole in one section of the brain that may or may not close," "possible mental retardation," "possible severe abnormalities."

She stated that our options included taking a risk in continuing the pregnancy, or we could choose to "terminate the kid." What was she saying! Her expression remained cold and clinical. She never made eye contact with me. She never looked to see the impact her words were having on me. She continued to speak those horrific words; all the while just over her left shoulder, the screen revealed our little girl still moving around.

I can't remember ever feeling then or now such raw fear and anger all at once. I wanted to scream, to punch her in that smug face. I wanted to save my baby. I jumped off the table with all the lubricating gel still on my belly—the belly where my little girl with the "hole in her brain" appeared to be happily sucking her thumb. I was halfway down the hall when I heard Jay's voice saying something loud and angry to Dr. J, who was responding that we were behaving irrationally. It was her job to…blah…blah…blah. The rest of her sentence could not and would not be heard.

We left the building and immediately went home to be with our family. They each said aloud what Jay and I already knew in our hearts. Whatever would be with this baby was out of our hands. We already loved her and would accept her "as is."

Our Sarah was born on schedule and perfect. The "hole" in her brain closed as it was meant to, and she is now an incredibly smart, beautiful, young twenty-year-old woman. I sometimes think about what would have happened if we had gotten pregnant on the schedule *we* wanted. We would not have Sarah. The flops and disappointments that accompanied the years of trying and failing at conceiving, and then the medical complications throughout the pregnancy, all needed to occur for us to be gifted with our daughter.

I have come to appreciate that the many gifts and wisdom that come from our flops and disappointments often guide or move us in directions on our life path, sometimes without us even knowing it. Past failures and disappointments seem to create an internal alarm system that consciously and subconsciously seems to guide our thinking and behavior. We are changed because of those failures. Every time we fail or are disappointed, we learn and develop awareness and often better skills to cope and creatively navigate through unfamiliar situations. We learn a tremendous amount about ourselves.

"It is our failures that give us the passion to push harder toward our purpose," Nana would say. We learn about our unique internal strengths that in the absence of our disappointments would perhaps never be revealed. So I say perhaps we should be celebrating our failures and disappointments, but we can still rebel against our aging arm flops.

3 | *Growing Up: Making the Big Girl Shoes Fit*

"Optimism is the faith that leads to achievement. Nothing can be done without hope or confidence."

— HELEN KELLER

A friend of mine who is a highly respected cardiovascular surgeon in her early forties—beautiful, talented, well-published, and in a successful practice—once confided in me that sometimes when she puts on her surgical cap and catches a glimpse of herself in the mirror, she feels like an imposter. I know she intellectually understands her great surgical talents and gifts but emotionally carries self-doubt that sometimes casts a shadow over her confidence.

Similarly, a patient of mine who is a professional athlete, despite the cheers from adoring fans that greet him when he steps out on the field, admits he still feels his talents are more a function of luck then a result of his years of hard training, his dedication to preparing for games, and his God-given genetic abilities. The feeling of being an imposter is shared by many talented and well-accomplished individuals, particularly successful women.

"You think, why would anyone want to see me again in a movie? And I don't know how to act anyway, so why am I doing this?'"

Meryl Streep

So when I admit that I too know the experience of sometimes feeling like an imposter, I realize that I am in great company not only with my amazing friend and my talented patient, but also with many others. I take pride in knowing that I have something in common with Meryl Streep and award-winning author Maya Angelou, both who have admitted to feeling this type of self-doubt at times.

"I have written eleven books, but each time I think, 'Uh oh, they're going to find out now. I've run a game on everybody, and they're going to find me out.'"

Award-winning author Maya Angelo

As matter of fact, apparently 70 percent of the population has experienced this feeling at one point or another. This feeling is even shared by two-thirds of the incoming freshman class at Stanford Business School, who raised their hands when asked, "How many of you in here feel that you are the one mistake that the admissions committee made?"

In the field of psychology, this description of self-doubt has been referred to as the "imposter syndrome." It is most often seen among high-achieving, successful women. It is that voice in our head that says, "Soon others will find out that I am not all that they think I am, that I don't possess all the talents they give me credit for…it was just luck or circumstance or good fortune that brought me to this level of success." For many people, as their career progresses and they gain greater responsibilities, the internal doubt increases as the cost of failing gets higher.

I don't wear a surgical cap, I don't wear a professional sports jersey, and I certainly don't grace a stage as Meryl Streep can, but I share that feeling of being an imposter at times when I slip into my "big girl shoes." It's a feeling that I am parading around in my mother's shoes that simply don't fit. It's the grown-up shoes worn by mature, responsible, capable women with great wisdom and authority. Most of the time and admittedly more often as I have gotten older, I am able to monitor my self-doubt and to realistically manage it to restore my sense of confidence and pride in myself. But during a recent breakfast with my dear friend and brilliant colleague, Debbie, I could feel my shoes getting too big and slipping off my heels when she suggested I should write my memoir. My memoir, what is she talking about. Memoirs are written by famous old people who are reflecting back over their incredible lives, for people who have accomplished great things or for people who can bring great insights to others through their stories. The voice in my head was screaming, "You are not accomplished enough for such a task. Maybe Debbie's been drinking or becoming demented or both."

I still think I am too young (isn't that funny for a fifty-year-old woman) and certainly not that accomplished to be writing a memoir. Memoirs are written by sophisticated and seasoned individuals. The thought of writing one gave me that familiar imposter feeling. The feeling that makes me feel insecure and incapable, knowing that others would surely see that while I look like an adult and a professional, I am just trying to be a grown-up by wearing big girl shoes.

My first real awareness of feeling like an imposter came in August 1988, a Tuesday morning at Henry Ford Hospital in Detroit, Michigan, the second day of my clinical internship. The first day was orientation, which consisted of sitting in a large auditorium gathering binder after large binder of useful information about the hospital, listening about our rotations from our many supervisors, participating in a basic tutorial on the computer system, and collecting maps to help us locate the cafeteria, the record room, and the morgue — in that order. However, nothing in that orientation could have prepared me for the first full clinical day.

I lived in the resident's apartment on the hospital grounds on the fifteenth floor, so I could see the back entrance to the ER and the windows to the ICU units from my bedroom. That was where my primary rotations would begin. The hospital was massive in size and from my window appeared simultaneously beautiful and intimidating. On that Tuesday morning, I woke early and quickly changed into my olive-colored dress and my gray pumps with sensible heels. I put on my white lab coat that had "Dr. Lori Stevic-Rust" embroidered over the left pocket. I put my pocket-size DSMIII manual (diagnostic bible for psychologists) and my laminated card with approved medical abbreviations into my pocket and clipped on my name tag. I was ready.

I arrived on the ICU floor to complete my first consultation on a cardiac transplant patient. The lights in the hallway seemed especially bright, and the sound of machines beeping seemed to mirror the pounding in my chest. My supervisor was Dr. Richard Portman, an elderly man with gray hair and glasses that he wore low on the bridge of his nose, making him appear regal. He was a well-respected physician who made interns and residents very nervous. I was certainly no exception. There he sat waiting for me at the nurse's station. I stepped behind the counter and positioned myself in the swivel seat next to him.

He opened up room three's chart. He proceeded to walk me through all the essential features of the chart: the lab section, the consult section, the history and physical, physician orders and notes, and finally the nurse's section. I tried desperately to remember all he was saying, but my heart was pounding so fast and my mouth felt dry. It was clear my nerves were getting the better of me. I had a fleeting thought of asking him for a Valium but thought better of it. He had just met me and it was still unclear to me whether or not he had a sense of humor. I knew he was a Pittsburgh Steelers fan and I found humor in that—being a Browns fan. I knew I had to get it together. Really, Lori? Thinking about football just before you enter the room of your first patient. Thank God Dr. Portman could not hear my thoughts. He was tipping his head and waiting for me to follow him into the patient's room. I followed him to the doorway. He then paused and motioned for me to go in first. I stepped into the room.

Lying in the bed was a frail man looking older than his stated age—that's how we describe people in the world of health care.

I guess it means we have a benchmark for how we think people at certain ages should look. Anyways, this gentleman was connected to so many machines with tubes coming from all parts of his body. I imagine he felt a lifetime older than his stated age. I tried to avoid taking in the entire scene, as it only contributed to the existing feeling of nausea I had been struggling with since I got out of bed. I positioned myself in a chair near his bed, and Dr. Portman sat off near the window, out of the patient's sight but directly in my peripheral vision.

I introduced myself and asked if I could ask him some questions. I found myself focusing on his eyes. It is still so striking to me how the eyes reveal so much if we really pay attention. His eyes were screaming, *I am so scared, I don't want to die.* But his voice could only muster quiet weak-sounding words. He was waiting for a cardiac transplant and hope for an organ seemed to be fading, as were his spirits. My job was to evaluate his depression and offer a treatment plan to alleviate his distress while he waited. No simple task. What did I know about waiting to die — about the fear he must be feeling?

I pushed on and began to ask him questions about how he was feeling, his fears, and his mood. I completed my assessment. I looked over at Dr. Portman, who sat quietly watching me. He then stood and approached the patient's bed. He began to speak in a slow and quiet voice, and then he reached out and touched the patient's hand — peace seemed to settle on the face of the frightened man lying in the bed.

I couldn't move. I was so struck by the kindness and warmth in Dr. Portman's voice. I felt his compassion, and I am quite certain the patient did as well. Where did that come from? I thought this was to be a clinical, follow-the-books, no-nonsense assessment. He touched the patient. His voice was gentle. He didn't use words like *mood*, but rather asked about his spirits and his comfort level. His hands were so gentle and methodical as he reached out and covered the tube-covered arm of the patient. Dr. Portman looked up at me over top of his glasses and motioned for us to leave.

When we exited the room, he was complimentary about my approach and my assessment. He went on to provide me with what I think was useful clinical feedback. Unfortunately, I could not hear him. I was too busy listening to my own voice in my head saying, "Oh my God, what just happened? What am I doing here? I'm a doctor? I'm wearing professional clothes and big girl shoes, but I feel like just a kid...soon they will see that I am too young to be doing this important and serious work. How is it that Dr. Portman doesn't see my shoes slipping off my heels as I walk? These shoes are for a real doctor, a real adult, and a real woman, not me...I'm just a kid! Oh my God, I am an imposter."

When I think back on this day and many others throughout my career as a young adult, I realize that once I learned to have the humility to walk in the shoes of others, which is not always an easy task, I grew in my own confidence. I began to feel comfortable in my own unique shoes. The shoes that allowed me to enter a patient's room armed with my clinical knowledge but also with my sense of humor. I learned to embrace the fact that I could be moved to tears or could hug a patient without feeling ashamed that this was what "young, inexperienced, touchy-feely psychologists do." It was what I do. I had to shake free from the messages I received from many of my older male supervisors about being stoic and keeping my emotions in check if I ever wanted to succeed as a psychologist. The longer I wore my big girl shoes, the more I came to realize that my supervisors gave me these messages because they were simply too uncomfortable with emotions—theirs or anybody else's. (That's the beauty of being a psychologist; we can interpret things any way we like and make it sound factual.) It worked for me. I learned to celebrate and embrace my skills and successes and to recognize my inadequacies.

Recently I ran across a photograph of my youngest daughter, Katelyn, when she was about four years old. She was so little, petite, blonde with light green eyes and always a mischievous grin. She was wearing my high-heeled shoes and standing in the ditch in our front yard with a bullfrog in her hands beaming from ear to ear. I remember that day. The air was cool, too cool for the open-toed pumps that she had selected; the leaves were begin-ning to fall and I stood in the driveway taking her photo (literally and mentally). I smiled at the two different sides of my daugh-ter's personality: the little girl who liked to dress up and at the same time thought nothing of keeping up with the boys in the neighborhood by fishing or catching frogs and all while wearing my high-heeled shoes.

On that particular morning, as I stood in the driveway watch-ing her, she began to approach me with the frog in hand, walking with her heels sliding in and out of my shoes. She was shuffling her feet, trying to keep the shoes on and determined not to drop the frog. She took great pride in wearing those "big girl shoes." Back then she loved wearing *my* big girl shoes. Today, at sev-enteen, I am quite sure that walking in my shoes is not top on her agenda. But if history repeats itself and I'm sure it will, there will come a day when she *will* walk in my shoes. I hope for her that the experiences will bring her new insights, confidence, and purpose, as it did for me when I stepped into my mother's and grandmother's shoes for the first time.

It is interesting to me that my symbolic image of being an imposter — of growing up and growing in wisdom and empathy and trying to feel accomplished — is my *shoes,* of all things. It's funny because with my weird feet, high arches, and curled toes, finding shoes that fit and actually stay on my feet is often quite difficult. But once they are mine, they mold to my strange feet and would never fit anybody else. I looked at my grandmother's shoes the other day and noticed that she too makes her shoes fit her and only her. She takes tissue and puts them in the heel of the shoe to make them soft, and she will sometimes poke holes in the straps to make her own fitting. I am confident that anybody actually wearing my shoes or hers would never feel quite right or comfortable. But still today slipping my feet in her shoes makes me feel warm and connected to her.

Growing up, my mother's fancy shoes were always neatly arranged in her closet, which smelled like her (you know, that smell of a mom…a mixture of her perfume and household clean-ing products). They were always of good quality, not necessarily designers, but always kept in good condition. My mother did not believe in wearing shoes in the house because of germs, so the bottoms were usually wiped and then placed in her closet. That is a whole other story or book.

As a little girl, I would put them on and walk around the house feeling as pretty as my mother and as grown up. Through my teenage years, those same shoes suddenly seemed outdated, old-fashioned, and at times an embarrassment. I would never be caught dead trying them on or certainly wearing them. It wasn't until I had my own children that suddenly her fancy shoes seemed more stylish to me; her run-around-town, beat-up shoes seemed practical and comfortable. My mother suddenly seemed more real to me.

Recently I looked into a mirror and caught a glance of my mother. The compliment was the fact that at seventy-seven years old, she is still a beautiful woman. At the same time, I feel a little fear, because I wonder *when* did I, become her. Don't we all say we will never be like our mothers, and then somehow, some-way, we hear her words coming out of our mouths? Her insights become shared with ours, and her wisdom becomes more apparent. I have grown in appreciation and gratitude for all that I now realize about her.

My mother and I look very much alike and share many qualities. I learned to be a compassionate and generous caregiver from her. I share a love for my family and our traditions, which is at her core. And we both have grown into an appreciation of each other's differences. After I put on my mother's shoes, it suddenly became that much harder to judge her, to lose patience with her, to believe that I knew all the right answers. It meant seeing that I too may have held the same beliefs and made the same life choices as she did if I had lived in her shoes.

My mother's gift to me has been unwavering support and pride. Throughout the years she always loved and appreciated my shoes. She never saw the worn-down heel or the bump created by my high arch; she would tell me how beautiful they looked. The shoes that I often selected were not her style, but she always seemed to acknowledge that they looked perfect for me. My mother never ignored the fact that she could see my shoes slipping off me at times. Instead she would find a way to give me back my confidence, which would wash away that self-doubt and make my shoes fit again. My shoes would never fit my mother nor do hers fit me. But having walked in them as a little girl and after I started wearing my own big girl shoes, I grew to appreciate how perfectly her shoes fit her.

Perhaps the art of aging is about learning to climb the generational ladder and having the courage to step into the shoes of those who came before. Stepping into somebody else's shoes requires humility and the willingness to see life's journey through their eyes with their thoughts, their history, and their limitations. It means becoming vulnerable and taking a risk that our own preconceived thoughts and judgments could be wrong.

Nana has always been proud of me for many things — for everything. But I think she is particularly proud that I chose a profession that allows me to get as much as I give. She maintains that when we listen to people's stories, we learn to be compassionate and patient. "When you understand people's lives, you understand why they make the choices they do and behave in the way they do. You just have to listen to their stories." The gift in return is that we realize something new about ourselves.

I have certainly learned over decades of listening to the stories of others that we all share themes in life. At the core of human beings is the desire to be loved, to show love, to feel valued and connected. We all want to know that we are here for a reason — that there is a purpose for our existence. The art of living is to discover that purpose and then to find the courage and passion to push through pain and failure to realize it.

Listening, really listening, requires that we mute our active filtering voice, which is already making assumptions and conclusions before we even enter into a conversation with another. It requires the ability to truly step into what is being said and hear the words and listen to the meaning while consciously monitoring our voice of bias and judgment. It is only then that we are really able to walk in somebody else's shoes.

I first met John on the orthopedic wing of the hospital. I had been consulted to evaluate his behavior, which the nursing staff described as "obnoxious and disruptive" to the unit.

I began to review his chart. He was a — I was about to say a middle-aged man — he was fifty-five years old. Scratch that. He was a young man in his middle fifties. The intake history stated that he had fallen off a ladder and had broken his leg. He was brought to the emergency room by ambulance. The social history section revealed he had no family. He lived alone. He had a history of alcohol abuse, non-compliant behavior, and depression. This information was received from his primary care doctor, who admittedly had only seen him once in his office about five years ago. John had not been forthcoming with the staff regarding his injury. There were speculations that he had been drinking when he fell — an assumption based on his history of drinking. However, his toxicology screen was negative. Concerns regarding possible self-neglect were also raised, given his appearance and attitude.

As I came down the hall toward his room, I heard him yelling at the nurse, "Bitch, if you think I am going to let you get near me with that needle, you are out of your fucking mind." She yelled back that his language was unacceptable and she turned on her heels and left the room. She glanced at me and said, "Good luck. He is a real son of a bitch." Inside I was thinking, "Why do I always get these calls late in the afternoon? If I need to move him to a psychiatric floor, I will probably have trouble getting a bed at this hour." It had been a long day, and I really just wanted to head home. Given what the staff had reported about him throwing all professionals out of his room in short order, I assumed this wouldn't take long. I started to think about what I should make for dinner.

I moved these thoughts to the back burner in my mind and entered the room. I found an unshaven man with noticeably poor hygiene sitting straight up in his hospital bed. Before he could open his mouth, I heard my voice saying, "Hi, I'm Dr. Stevic-Rust and sometimes I do think I am out of my fucking mind, but I hope you will be patient with me anyway. I have no needles — not even a pen unfortunately. So I guess I will have to rely on my memory. May I sit down for a few minutes?"

He nodded but quickly asked, "What the hell kind of doctor are you?" Oh, the dreaded question. I answered, "Not a real one—I'm just a psychologist." I really believe John desperately wanted to avoid smiling, but somehow my charm overwhelmed him. I always knew that the F-word would come in handy one day—despite how much my mother and grandmother both disapproved of the vile word. Slowly I began to ask about what happened to him...I listened, only listened, to what became a two and-a-half-hour story.

The highlights of the story were in such stark contrast to what his life looked like on paper in the medical chart. He was an alcoholic who quit drinking two years ago on his own and almost died from withdrawal, but was afraid to seek out medical care because of shame over being a drunk. His wife left him four years ago and took his three kids to "protect them from seeing me drunk and out of work. I am a real embarrassment—a loser. I don't blame her for leaving," he added. His only companion was his eighty-two-year-old neighbor who would bring him meals after his wife left. His neighbor then suffered a stroke and he had been trying to help her remain in her home over the past year. She was afraid the state would put her in a nursing home. He was sharing his limited financial resources with her. Subsequently, his own electricity had been turned off the week prior and he had no running water—hence the disheveled appearance. He fell off the ladder when he was trying to fix a light over her garage.

He went on to admit that he had a tremendous fear of hospitals. When he was a young boy, he watched his mother die from cancer in a hospital. He had suffered post-traumatic stress symptoms since that time, including flashback images of her frail body in the hospital bed with tubes hanging out of her. He began suffering panic attacks and intense anxiety when seeing needles or hearing stories of those who were physically sick. Generalized anxiety took over and ultimately led to compulsions to manage his anxiety.

In his midthirties he began to drink to manage the anxiety. Eventually the anxiety and fear of germs and getting sick became so intense; they began to interfere with his ability to work. He began avoiding public restrooms and started compulsively washing his hands hundreds of times a day to prevent getting sick. He lost several jobs as a result. He ended up on disability and the shame of "not being a man" appeared to be feeding his depression.

Briefly walking through the story of John's life, walking in his shoes for a moment, and seeing what the hospital room and the staff represented to him quieted my own biases. I did not need to find a psychiatric bed for John. I needed to help him manage his fears and anxiety about hospitals, the staff, and his own mother's death. I needed to help the staff understand John's fears. He acted in quite an obnoxious way to push the staff away from him. He operated out of his own fear and not some hatred or mean-spirited attitude toward the staff. His insecurities, fears, and depression revealed themselves as anger and self-neglect.

My ability and willingness to see the world through his eyes, to empathize with him, gave me perspective about myself. When I stepped out in the hallway and back into my own shoes, I realized John and I had a few things in common. While I cannot drink more than the neck of a beer before breaking into my own rendition of Tom Jones's "What's New Pussycat?" and I can't stand the idea of going a day without showering, I can become defensive and angry when I am scared or feel insecure. It is protective. My behavior and attitude on occasion has even led to me being called a fucking bitch and much more—and *once* it was even deserved. That's a story for another time.

As a culture, we are self-centered and self-absorbed, but in the end the truth is we all share more in common than we would at times like to admit. It is through empathy, a willingness to see things through the perspective of others that we truly learn about ourselves. I am not naïve to think that we get rid of our biases or our judgments of others, but empathy brings the ability to be mindful of how our biases operate. I become more self-aware every time I step into somebody else's shoes. I am comfortable walking around with my known judgments and biased views because with the awareness of them, I have the ability to manage them, to challenge them, and to ultimately change them.

As a psychologist I have had the great privilege and opportunity of walking in the shoes of others, which has made me more comfortable *wearing* my own.

4 | Rooted to Our Family Traditions

"Whatever else be lost among the years, Let us keep Christmas still a shining thing: Whatever doubts assail us, or what fears, Let us hold close one day, remembering Its poignant meaning for the hearts of men. Let us get back our childlike faith again."

— GRACE NOLL CROWELL

It was still dark, but the light from the streetlamp was casting a shadow through the sheer drapes and across the floor where I was lying. The blue blanket covering my feet was twisted up, but just beyond the mound it created, I could see them. Toys, toys everywhere; I could see the game of Clue standing up tall facing me, with a twirling top made of every color of the rainbow sitting just behind it. I rolled over and nudged my sister Leanne, who was lying on the floor next to me. But she was already awake, whispering, "There it is, there it is." I followed where her hand was pointing and just past her head on the floor was the royal-blue Little Tike teeter totter.

He came. He came. Santa had been there the night before. And just as it was in all the years before, he somehow had snuck into Grandma and Grandpa's house, climbed around my sister and I, who were sleeping on the floor, and had gently placed gifts all around us, under the Christmas tree, and next to the couch

31

where my older sister, Diane, was sleeping. She would sleep on the couch because she was the oldest. I think she thought this made her special, but truth be told, I simply felt sorry for her because sleeping on the floor under the tree surrounded by all those toys was magic.

Once we were awake, Leanne and I were faced with a difficult decision. Did we pretend that we hadn't seen the toys that were clearly visible and try to go back to sleep until a reasonable time when everybody else in the house would be awake? Should we wake Diane to see the gifts? Well, clearly there was no going back to sleep and waking Diane was a frightening concept as she had already shaken and examined her wrapped gifts the night before and pretty much knew exactly what was in each. So she would probably not be thrilled getting up before the sun. Diane, who is six years older than I am and ten years older than Leanne, clearly took charge of these situations, and of us, for that matter; therefore, we were clearly not going to risk being threatened or intimidated into going back to sleep. Instead, we took the logical approach and ran to the back bedrooms to wake our parents and grandparents.

It was Christmas morning and like every year, we spent it sleeping on the gold-carpeted living room floor of my grandparents' home. There were two green sofas and my grandfather's Archie Bunker chair. You know the kind, with the stuffing coming out from years of wear and the shape of the cushions molded to his body shape—round. Consistent with my grandfather's need to "doctor things up," the leather chair had duct tape covering a hole in the right arm. It also had some green epoxy holding one of the legs together. My grandfather loved epoxy and put it on anything and everything, but secretly, to avoid the fight with my grandmother.

The living room walls were covered in floral wallpaper that surrounded the artificial fireplace. And by artificial I mean a fireplace with the woodburning log that you plug in and the fake brick front—but it was where Santa would come down, so it was the best fireplace ever. As a matter of fact, ten years ago when my grandmother sold the house, it was the last thing I looked at before we closed the door. That fireplace was the center of Christmas morning, and it held so many of my most cherished memories.

Santa never wrapped gifts. He simply took them from his sack off the sleigh and placed them all around us as we slept. This was also how you knew they were from him and not Mom and Dad, because theirs were wrapped. Santa's gifts were special and did not need to be wrapped. It could also be that we lived in Ashtabula growing up and my grandparents lived in Akron, and we never celebrated Christmas morning in our home. That meant my parents or Santa (I'm still not willing to acknowledge it was my parents) had to transport all the gifts in a car filled with kids without their knowledge, or it may have simply meant that gifts were purchased in Akron and there was no time to wrap. I still really don't know the truth about how this task was accomplished. I refuse to ruin the magic of the memory by knowing.

The Christmas ornaments and tree were kept in the basement, or as my grandparents called it, the cellar. Actually, it really was a cellar. It had a ceiling so low that at five foot three, I felt the need to duck down when I entered. The floor was concrete and the rafters were made of old wood and copper pipes. Clotheslines ran from one end of the basement to the other. Why these stick out in my mind is because on many days during my college years, I would go down to the cellar to do laundry and would be confronted by rabbits, or whatever had been hunted by my grandfather and uncle, "drying" on the lines. Always an unpleasant sight but complaining about it only brought comments like "don't be so sensitive" and "dinner will be ready in a couple of hours." On those special dinner nights, I cooked for myself and made the excuse of lots of homework. Who wants to eat what was hanging from the clothesline?

Images of the hanging carcasses often were replaced by the other incredible things that occurred in that cellar. This is where we as an entire family canned the tomatoes. Any good Italian family knows about the canning of the tomatoes. It begins with the process of laying tomatoes on newspapers until the entire basement was covered. This was then followed by each of us kids using our little red wagon to wheel the tomatoes to the stationary tub, where we would gently place them in the water for cleaning. This was followed by the cooking, seeding, peeling, and jarring process. If successful, the jars would "sing" and this meant that they were sealed. While we kids would wait for the jars to sing, we often would sneak into the fruit cellar, which was another little cellar inside the cellar. It was dark and smelled musty and old, but inside that room were tall cardboard bins with metal lids that housed all the magical Christmas ornaments. Behind them stood the tall box where the Christmas tree was kept. But my favorite of all was the big plastic bin with the special green wrapping paper that covered the nativity set. Just looking at the bins was exciting, knowing their contents would soon light up the living room again.

The Christmas tree was traditionally put up by my grandfather. This is the grandfather who by his own admission was grumpy and rough on the outside. The last thing you would imagine was this guy taking time to put up a tree or have an interest in having the tree at all. But he did it in a big way. It was my grandmother who was a bit of scrooge into this issue. She always felt that he wanted to put it up too early, and he felt that she took too long to get in the spirit, so he would do it while she was at work. I was often pulled into the middle of this argument. I was always of the belief that it was never too early to begin to enjoy a time of year that always made our house smell and feel like family.

The Christmas tree was artificial, with the old branches that had to be placed piece by piece into the wooden trunk. My grandfather would take hours to complete this task. He would then proceed with the lights. How they were placed on the tree was irrelevant; whether or not the ornaments hung in a symmetrical fashion, it made no difference. If things were falling or didn't fit, he would use his green epoxy to make them stay.

When the lights on the manger were too dim, he decided that more shining from the roof would be better, so he drilled big holes and put large lights in the roof. Poor baby Jesus, Mary, and Joseph they looked like they were being interrogated under the bright lights. But he was happy with his work. He would hang random lights over the fireplace and buy "extra" lighted objects of Santa or reindeer from the local drugstore. This would drive my grandmother crazy and would often lead to fights. But to me the tree was magical. I loved how the lights glistened at night when we lay under it in the dark, how the tinsel hung, and how the ornamental electric candles bubbled on the tree branches. Grandpa had succeeded; the living room was transformed with a feeling of excitement and warmth.

My grandmother's parents came from Poland and my grandfather's family from Italy. So, we all reaped the benefit of having a Polish grandmother who brings rich traditions and great food from her family of origin, but who also had the good sense to marry an Italian man with sisters who loved to cook. My grandmother was the Polish farm girl who had to learn to speak Italian to communicate with her in-laws and most importantly to learn their secret recipes. She became the great Polish-Italian cook and so did my mom and my sisters and me. We love our food and our deep traditions.

The most sacred and deepest tradition in our family comes from my grandmother's Polish heritage, and that is the Christmas Eve celebration of Wigilia (pronounced Vilia). It is the most solemn and spiritual part of our Christmas celebrations. Days in advance of the meal, my mother will prepare the table. She places hay under the white tablecloth to symbolize Christ in the manger, and she sets an empty plate. Traditionally, this is meant to be symbolic, representing Christ in our presence or the welcoming of a stranger. However with my family, most times it isn't symbolic. It never surprises any of us to find that my mother has invited third-cousin Tina's mailman to join us or the lady from the produce section at Giant Eagle, who is widowed with no place to spend Christmas Eve.

In preparation, my mother would also purchase the Oplatek, which is the traditional wafer that is blessed by a priest. The Christmas Eve tradition begins with waiting for the first star to be seen; this commemorates the birth of Christ and is the sign that the meal can begin. We all hold hands and my mother leads us in a prayer, which gives her an opportunity to express gratitude for us all being together as a family and for our health. We then each take a piece of the Oplatek and break a small piece from one another's bread and share a piece from our own. We exchange thoughts of love and gratitude for one another and then move to the next person. At the end everyone will have shared a piece of his own blessed wafer (known as the bread of love) and have eaten a piece from each family member. This tradition has been occurring since I was a little girl, and still it brings everybody to tears.

Now as beautiful as all of that is, the meal is not what kids or picky eaters would enjoy. It is a meatless meal that consists of several different types of fish, spaghetti with oil and onions, soup, and our traditional smelt fish. These are frequently referred to as the "dried pieces of shit." They are hard, dry, and tasteless, but for fear of bad karma or family ridicule, we eat them — at least we choke down one, or take one bite, which we may later spit out.

In our family we tend to believe that traditions can be mixed. We think Santa and Jesus can be celebrated together. In fact, my grandfather once found at Woolworth's a ceramic figurine of a Native American on a horse. Every year he would place it near the manger among the three wise men. We don't really know why he thought this worked, but we never questioned it. The manger with the drilled holes in the ceiling and the chipped figures and the Native American are all proudly displayed every year on my kitchen counter at Christmas. I think of my grandfather when I turn the lights on.

These traditions are so rooted in the generations before me and are so deeply cherished and maintained by my family today. With that said, and with no shame or embarrassment, I admit that I currently begin to decorate for Christmas in November. OK, not really the day after Thanksgiving, but near the first week of November and only because my family holds me back from doing it in October. When you enter our home at Christmas, you will typically see a seventeen-foot live tree. Every year we complain about the mess it creates. The needles in between the hardwood floor pieces are sometimes still being sucked up in the vacuum a year later. Just in time for the fresh tree to be put up. But the tradition of getting the tree and smelling the fresh pine pushes our old bones forward each year on the hunt for the perfect tree.

When the girls were little, we would take them out to a farm to cut down the tree. They would each get into their snowsuits, boots, and mittens and begin to follow their dad into the woods. I was always busy picking up whatever kid fell, replacing the gloves that came off, and yelling for them not to get too close to the saw. And then we would find that perfect tree. Jay would lie in the snow and cut the tree down while the girls and I would clap, unable to offer any other assistance. He would drag the tree back to the little barn for the staff to wrap and place on the roof of the car. The girls and I would drink hot chocolate and watch the process through the window of the warm barn.

Our girls are now twenty and seventeen, but the tradition of getting a live tree continues. However, it has changed a bit. Now when we go, they take their cell phones so we can all divide up to locate the perfect tree and then text one another when we find it. We skip the hot chocolate because we usually stop at Starbucks on the way to bring our own chai tea. Jay still has to lie on the ground to cut the tree, but this past year the girls were concerned about him trying to carry it alone, so they hoisted the tree onto a sled and helped him pull it back to the barn. They helped him tie and load the tree onto the roof. But when the tree gets comfortably into the stand in our home, we do not break with tradition. Everybody goes their separate ways until I have strategically placed all sixteen hundred lights onto the tree. They say it's because I do such a nice job and I believe them.

As if this monster of a tree is not enough, there is also an artificial rotating nine-foot tree in our foyer, twenty-one "small" white lit trees on the ledge of the stairs, two "themed" eight-foot trees in the basement, and each of my daughters decorates her own room with trees, hanging lights, manger sets, and so forth. The house sparkles and is filled with such joy. But it is not just my home. You could enter either of my sisters' homes, my mother's home, or my two nieces' homes and would see a similar scene. OK, maybe not as many trees as I have, but the spirit of Christmas and the depth of our traditions would still be felt. The gifts from Santa are still not wrapped; the trees in each of my girls' rooms and my nieces all hold ornaments passed down through the generations; and the smell of traditional cookies is the same in all of our homes.

Traditions in our family just don't die. As a matter of fact, when my sister Diane had the nerve to move out of town ten years ago, we all learned to adjust to mailing birthday gifts, texting more often, and even adjusting vacation schedules to spend time together. But the hardest thing for all of us was to adjust to not always being together for Christmas. Another one of our traditions on Christmas Eve that follows the Wigilia meal is that we all, adults and children, bring our pajamas to my parents' house and put them on while my husband reads *The Polar Express*.

This tradition started before Jay and I had any children of our own. We would sleep at my sister Diane's house on Christmas Eve so we could be with my nieces when they woke up to Santa's gifts in the morning. We slept on the pullout coach in the living room, and they would climb in with us before going to bed, and he would read *Twas the Night Before Christmas*. As the years went by, this became an important tradition for them. As we all started to have children, it became a deeply cherished tradition. One year my niece Stephanie made blankets for all the cousins. So before Uncle Jay would read, everybody would get into their pajamas, grab their "Stephanie blanket," and then snuggle all around Uncle Jay. Years ago *The Polar Express* book was chosen because we decided as a family that secretly we all still hear the "bell ringing," because we do still believe — believe in the incredible power of sharing a family tradition that makes us all feel so connected to one another. And in Santa...of course.

My nieces are now thirty-one and twenty-eight years old (wow, another realty check about my aging), and they have families of their own, but our traditions remain. Every Christmas Eve after our Wigilia dinner, we still put on our pajamas, including

Nana. We grab our "Stephanie blankets," we snuggle by Uncle Jay, and then we turn on different laptops to Skype to Myrtle Beach and to Florida. The reading of *The Polar Express* is now shared with five generations in three different states.

Why do we eat smelts, maintain Santa gifts, and put out the ornaments from generations before? I think the answer is that living our traditions brings us closer to the core of who we are as a family. It connects us to our generations. The stories we create, the feelings we share, and the hopes we hold for one another define the life that we have lived as a family. It is uniquely ours.

5 | *The Women in My Family: Born and Bred Caregivers*

"How far you go in life depends on your being tender with the young, compassionate with the aged, sympathetic with the striving and tolerant of the weak and the strong. Because someday in life you will have been all of these."

—GEORGE WASHINGTON CARVER

We are a family of girls. My mother had three girls; my oldest sister, Diane, had three girls; and I had two girls. So when my youngest sister, Leanne, was told she was having identical twins, the doctor asked if she wanted to know the sex of the twins. We all laughed and said, "We already know they are girls." And they were. It took my oldest niece, Jennifer, to break the mold and provide this family with not one, but three little boys. However, after the first ultrasound, we were skeptical when the doctor told her he saw a penis. We all thought he could be wrong; after all, we don't do boys—even our dogs are female or neutered males. Thank God Jennifer did break that mold because now I have three of the sweetest great-nephews. I am Great-Aunt Lori, and I choose to think of that as a descriptive title, not a reflection of my age.

My mother-in-law had three boys, and I often heard her lamenting over not having a daughter. She loved her boys but believed that girls tended to stay closer to their families and seemed to be the caregivers for the emotional and physical needs of each generation. I don't have a point of reference for this, with no brothers and no sons, but I can speak to the fact that I am a product of generations of caregivers. Is that because we are women or because we have been given the gift of being raised by caring and nurturing human beings who believe in the value of caring for others? I think the latter.

In fact I have come to believe that perhaps being kind, generous caregivers may not only be inherited but also sexually transmitted. All of the men in our family understand and embrace the art of caring for others. My father, Bill, showed me how gently and loving a man can really be. While he sadly admits he was raised in a family that had tendencies to be more selfish and self-centered, he believes that marrying my mother taught him about caring for others. All of his daughters and granddaughters don't buy that explanation. We all know that at the core of my father's being is a man who is all about, "How can I help?" He is the man who can always figure out how something can be done and intuitively knows when others need him to do it.

My maternal great-grandparents lived in the hills of Pennsylvania; at the time when my parents were first married, they had no running water in the house. It bothered my father to see my mother's elderly grandparents carrying buckets of water into the house. So he tapped into a mountain stream and plumbed a line into the house for running water. He built three of his own homes and helped with two of mine, despite not being an architect or a builder. When we were little and we didn't feel well at night, he did not send my mother while he slept. He came with my mother to get us ginger ale, hot water bottles, or to simply sit on our bed until we fell asleep. He changed the diapers of the grandchildren and now his great-grandchildren. He is the man who helps in the day-to-day care of our Nana. He makes her coffee every morning, helps her in and out of the car, stays with her when my mother needs a break, and does all of this and more in his usual sensitive and loving way.

It is not surprising then to know that each of us girls selected husbands much like our father. What a compliment to them.

My brothers-in-law not only care for their own families but also provide love and support to our extended family. They are the first to step up to help care for my grandmother, or as they genuinely feel, *their* grandmother.

I think my mother-in-law was wrong in her assessment that boys don't take care of their families in the same way that girls do. I would argue that her son Jay did not learn to be a caregiver from me. He came to me as a caregiving person. He too helps with all the big caregiving needs for Nana and our family, but he can also make a room full of people feel loved and important with all of the small caring things he does.

Several years after Jay and I were married, we took a trip to Punxsutawney, Pennsylvania, home of the famous groundhog and where my mother grew up. While we were there, we met an old neighbor of my grandparents. We sat on her front porch and drank lemonade, and I learned many things about my grandparents.

She took a deep breath and said softly, "I had five children when I lived next to your grandparents. One year when my husband lost his job, your grandparents paid our mortgage for two months and bought the kids shoes so they wouldn't be ashamed to start school with shoes that had holes in them." I could see her fighting back tears. She went on to say that she knew they helped other families by providing meals to them when money was tight. We heard endless stories of selfless and at times anonymous acts of caregiving by my grandparents.

I learned later that in order for my grandparents to give as they did, they had to cut into their own food budget and pull money out of their savings to pay the neighbor's mortgage. This was only one of many stories of generosity and selfless giving that we heard. My cousins who still live in the town told us that because of the kindness and caregiving that my grandparents showed, they were rewarded with loyalty and support from the town. Whenever possible the town would patronize my grandparents' restaurant, the Quick Lunch. The business became successful, and staying consistent with their character, my grandparents shared that success with many other families in need, particularly if the need involved hunger. They could not tolerate the idea that people would go to bed hungry or children would go to school with no lunch. Once a week they would open the restaurant and allow people to pay what they could for their meal. My grandparents set the expectations for the tradition of caregiving for generations that would follow.

When I was a junior in high school, my Aunt Joan (my grandmother's third-youngest sister) came to live with us. She had advanced emphysema and other related medical conditions from years of really, really enjoying life. She came from the same poor family that my grandmother did, raised on a farm with sixteen brothers and sisters, but she may as well have been from another planet, based on the night-and-day differences between her and my grandmother. Fredrick Collins said, "There are two kinds of people. Those who enter a room and say, 'Well, here I am.' And then those who come in and say, "Ah, there you are.'" My grandmother is the latter, and Aunt Joan was clearly the former.

She weighed all of about ninety pounds, but her attitude weighed twice that. She had the same fair skin and light hair color as my grandmother. She had the barreled chest appearance that many patients develop with lung disease. When she entered a room, she seemed to strut in, chest out, nose high; her arms swung disproportionately fast. Her body language said, "Here I am." Actually, I think her body and her mouth would say that.

She called everybody "doll." What are you eating, doll? Where have you been, doll? And then there were the hand gestures. She spoke with her hands often in the shape of a claw. She would motion into the air for affect, with her fingers and her thumb touching and then opening as if she were reaching for something. Aunt Joan turned out to be a funny, odd, entitled, and ornery woman that over time we all developed affectionate feelings for—but the start was rocky.

Aunt Joan (real name Tophila—but changed to be more sophisticated) married a wealthy man twenty years her senior from New York City. After his death and a significant change in her financial lifestyle, she moved back to Akron to be near her family so they could take care of her.

I never knew I had an Aunt Joan. She was never around for holidays, birthdays, or when any of us were sick. But there she was sitting at our kitchen table one day when I came home from school. My mother shared with us privately that she needed somebody to take care of her because she could not live alone. I remember thinking, but why us. Truth. I rarely thought things quietly back in those days or in the present day. I said it out loud to my mother. Her response was because that's what family does for each other. It was a nice sentiment, but I was hoping this new intrusion into our home wasn't going to inconvenience us; and by us I meant me. I was sixteen and needed my freedom.

And life as a caregiver began. One day we all went to a restaurant called the Barn. It was chosen because of the décor, which was rustic in an upscale way, and had replicas of expensive horse saddles and photos of professional thoroughbreds on the wall. Aunt Joan liked going because she often said it was the only restaurant in Ohio that made steaks close to the way they were made in New York. "Close to" was the operative word, as nothing was ever as good as New York.

When we arrived at the restaurant, she demanded to have the chef come to the table. She gave him specific instructions on how her steak was to be prepared and she insisted that the raw piece of meat be brought to the table so she could approve the quality. I wanted to, or maybe I did, climb under the table to avoid being seen with her. If dining out had been the only embarrassment, perhaps it would have been easier to manage. I would simply make excuses about dining out. But Aunt Joan's charm permeated the home as well. One day my boyfriend came over after school and without warning she reached over and grabbed my left breast, announcing to all that they still had not successfully grown. Actually, she said, "These are the smallest tits I have ever felt." This was my Aunt Joan.

She stayed with us for two years, and although my mother was insulted on a regular basis by Aunt Joan and inconvenienced by her care needs most days, she cared for her out of compassion and respect for my grandmother. My mother knew that if she didn't provide the care, my grandmother would, simply because it was her sister and that's what families do. We all learned to share in her care. My sister Leanne would cut her nails, clean her oxygen machine, or as she referred to it, "the green hornet." We think she called it this because of the green hosing, but with Aunt Joan it was anybody's guess.

I was the one who would assist her in the middle of the night with her nosebleeds. I would pack her nose and apply pressure for hours until it would stop. This was my caregiving task because my room was across from hers, and I typically was the first to hear her call. I was also responsible for making the weekly run to the store to buy her Russell Stover Little Ambassador candies. How do I remember the type of candy after thirty-two years? Because if I bought the wrong chocolates, she would insist that I return for the right kind. And we all did really agree that the Little Ambassadors were the best-tasting chocolates.

On first glance, it seems odd to me that stories of Aunt Joan should make it into my memoirs. But as I reflect back how my parents graciously cared for her and encouraged and modeled for us how to do the same despite her difficult style, I realize I learned to see Aunt Joan through a different pair of eyes. I learned to accept her eccentricities and her rough style as nothing more than that of a lonely woman with no children, no husband, and only us to care about her. She was scared and hung on so desperately to the image of whom she was to avoid seeing the frail, ill, elderly person she had become. It was the first time I remember looking not at someone's behavior, but at the reasons why she behaved as she did. I learned tolerance. Perhaps it was Aunt Joan who set my feet firmly on the path of becoming a psychologist. What a thought.

I think my sister Leanne and I both learned a lot about empathy, and we lost some of the self-absorbed and selfish tendencies that naturally come with being a teenager during those years we spent with Aunt Joan. Although today we all laugh to think perhaps we could have learned that life lesson on somebody easier to care for, like — well, just about anybody.

The revolving front door of my parents' home welcomed my paternal grandmother to live with them after her stroke. This was followed by our dear Nana, who now lives with them. She moved in with them about ten years ago at the age of ninety. She stays with me a couple of months out of the year while my parents visit my sister and nieces who live out of town, and she comes to stay with us several weekends to simply hang out.

Caregiving is in our blood and in our souls. It is a shared family opportunity to provide care. I don't believe we do this because we are women. My father, my husband, and my brothers-in-law all share in the caregiving, as do my daughters and my nieces. They all share in the physical care and the emotional worry, and they demonstrate genuine love. My daughters take Nana to the store, to get her hair done, to pick apples. They spend hours talking to her and listening to her stories. They check on her in the night when they hear her coughing or getting up.

There isn't one of us from the four generations who would say that providing care isn't work, because it is. We would all agree that at times the responsibility and daily needs can become overwhelming and we need to take a break. However, we would all agree that admitting that makes us feel guilty. We would all agree that we could not be true caregivers if we didn't take care of ourselves and one another. But there isn't one of us who wouldn't agree that being caregivers to different generations has taught us more about ourselves than anything else we could ever do.

Caregiving seems to bring out the best in all of us, despite how exhausting it can be. We all fully appreciate how blessed we are to have five generations. What a unique and amazing gift. The connectivity to our generations allows us to look up and back at the same time. We are transformed. This became crystal clear to me one day when I overheard a conversation between Nana and my girls. What was happening at the dinner table was transformative, far more than any of my lecturing and modeling could have ever accomplished. Nana was sharing a secret family story and in the process was teaching my girls about history and gratitude.

It was Saturday and Nana was staying with us. The day was cloudy and rainy with no hope for sunshine in the forecast. I had just popped another load of laundry into the dryer when I came into the kitchen and heard Nana and my girls chatting at the kitchen table. The leftover lunch plates were still on the table. Katie had her feet up on the chair next to her with her cell phone sitting on the table (to avoid missing an important tweet). Sarah sat across from Katie and next to Nana. Nana was sitting on the tall bar stool chairs that made her legs dangle. She was swinging them back and forth to keep the circulation moving, but the gesture made her look young and carefree.

"It was one of the most painful times in our family's life," Nana was saying. "My oldest sister, Jenny, was walking to school one day. She would cut through the woods as we all did, since it was the closest route to school. We never worried about safety back then. The only thing we ever worried about was some of the other kids, who would push us down and call us names like hayseeders."

"What did that mean?" Katie asked.

"It was what they called us because we were poor farmers," Nana said. "I didn't care when they said it to me, but I hated when they picked on Stanley, my younger brother, who was small. One day I waited for those boys after school, and I hit them over the head with my metal lunch bucket and told them if they ever pushed Stanley down again, I would give them some more."

Sarah laughed until she snorted. "That's my Nana."

Nana dropped her voice and added, "I wish I would have been there the day that Jenny took the shortcut through the woods, and that old bastard from town grabbed her and forced sex on her. She was sixteen years old, and he was a fifty-one-year-old man who was a father of three children of his own. Jenny never told anybody. I know now that she was so ashamed and thought maybe it was her fault. She knew everybody liked and knew this man, and they probably wouldn't believe a farm girl like her.

"Jenny and I shared a bed, and at night I would hear her crying, but she wouldn't say why. Things were busy in our house because my mom was about to have her seventeenth child. As one of the oldest daughters, I knew it would be my job to help with the new baby. It turned out that Jenny was going to have a baby too. But none of us knew."

"Didn't anybody notice that she was getting big?" Sarah asked. "How could somebody be pregnant and nobody realize?"

"She wore big baggy sack dresses like the rest of us," Nana said. "But truth is I don't think any of us wanted to see it. That would be such a shame."

"What do you mean a shame?" Katie yelled. "She was raped. It wasn't her fault."

Nana's voice got even lower. "That was the shit of our times. Women didn't matter in the way they do today and certainly not poor farm women. Who would believe her? Worse, my own father didn't believe her. He ended up birthing Jenny's baby at our home just three days after my mother gave birth to my brother Joseph.

"After Jenny's baby was born, my father physically threw Jenny out of the house and called her a whore. She tried to explain what happened, but it didn't matter. She was forbidden from ever coming back to the house. He felt she had brought shame to the family — to him. My father said he would take care of the baby but not her. She was sixteen years old, Katie — younger than you. Jenny moved into a house with a family in town, where she served as their housekeeper. I used to sneak the baby up to the end of the driveway near the mailbox so Jenny could see him. Being a woman and living during my generation was not easy. How wonderful that woman in my time fought back and changed things for girls like you today. Don't take that for granted — remember that."

The heaviness of Nana's story hit hard. The conversation went on with more details filled in and more outrage expressed by my girls. The stories continued and morphed into a discussion on the importance of tolerance and sensitivity and human rights. I heard Sarah talking about her involvement on her college campus with a leadership group that focused on treating people with dignity and fighting for human rights and choices. She was explaining to Nana how social media is changing the way we communicate on these important issues.

The next thing I knew, the laptop was out on the table, and Sarah and Katie were both showing Nana how Twitter works.

How you can click on links on YouTube to view clips of media from anything you want. As I glanced up from the dishes I was doing at the kitchen sink, I saw Nana laughing and engaged. She was learning from two generations below her, and she was emotionally reaping the benefits of her interaction with them. The girls were learning firsthand what it was like to be a young woman in the late 1920s, and Nana was learning how to tweet and watch YouTube videos.

The girls opened up a video clip from President Obama showing him talking about supporting gay marriages. Nana looked at the girls.

"I have never been more proud of a president," she said. "He says what he feels without worrying about what is popular. I don't really understand gay relationships much, but I do think we should never assume to know what is right for another person. I don't think legal rights should just be for white people who have money."

Sarah looked at me and mouthed, "What the heck?" I had a front-row seat to watch the stereotypes of our different generations shatter apart. If I had asked my twenty-year-old and seventeen-year-old daughters prior to this conversation if they thought a woman of Nana's generation would hold liberal thoughts and views, they clearly would have said no. Their assumption of old-fashioned elderly folks would have been of conservative beliefs that they perhaps could not relate to in any meaningful way. They were changed. The first steps had been taken to open their minds to the possibility that there is much to learn from the generations before them.

Reaching up two and three generations before them for guidance and insight was far less threatening than hearing it from me. I am only one generation above them and a mother, no less—far too threatening to listen to me. It is natural to rebel against parents. It is part of the normal rites of passage through the developmental stages to think your parents are stupid and out of touch. It is less threatening to be drawn in to listen to the face of a "sweet old person," but what my girls may have been thinking was just going to be a lunch conversation with old Nana turned into a life lesson that was deeply planted in them.

They heard her wisdom, her biases, and her fears. They heard her voice. It was a message of hardship for women that they will not have to experience because other woman before them did. It was a message of tolerance and remaining open-minded to the rights and needs of people that perhaps you can't understand or even agree with. It was her voice that they would reflect on for years to come — that I was certain.

Lunch ended, and Nana's dangling legs were getting tired. The girls both grabbed each side of her and eased her off the bar-stool. Sarah guided her walker to her, and Katie took her water off the table, refilled it, and placed it next to her seat on the couch. The caregiving routine was engrained. Everybody knew her part — nobody had to be asked or reminded.

Our intergenerational daily life continues. It is part of who we are. That is probably why when we are in public, none of us ever hesitate to offer a hand to an elderly person who may be struggling to get up from a restaurant table, and why my crabby teenage girls exercise tremendous patience when driving behind an elderly person. It is second nature — no, it is now our primary nature to treat the generations above us with respect and gratitude and always in a way to preserve their dignity — they earned it.

Because while we are all gentle, kind, loving people, when somebody in public refers to Nana as "sweetie" or "cutie," we become vicious attack dogs. It makes Nana laugh. We don't see the humor. It is probably because we have taken the time to learn Nana's stories and have developed a deep appreciation for all the complexities of the person behind the one-hundred-year-old face and body. "Sweetie" and "honey" are words of endearment for children, not for our bright, funny, gifted, and incredibly wise Nana. We have been transformed through our lives as caregivers to appreciate that behind the old faces of our elderly are similar stories of heroism, strength, intellect, and kindness that need to be respected through our actions and the words and tone we use when we greet them.

"When you take care of others, you sleep better at night," Nana reminds us. "You realize you are here for a purpose. You were needed." I could not think of a better life lesson for my girls to have learned. What a gift to be generational caregivers.

6 | *Nana's Table*

"We live not by things, but by the meaning of things. It is needful to transmit the passwords from generation to generation."

— ANTOINE DE SAINT EXUPÉRY

The boxes in the kitchen, the storage bins of clothes in the hallway, and the piles of sheets and towels in the laundry room were reminders that my oldest daughter, Sarah, was heading back to college. Since this is her second year, I think of myself as a somewhat "seasoned college mom," which is why my level of sadness at her leaving this year caught me off guard. It may have been that preparing for her to leave for her first year of college was surprisingly easy. She was so excited and eager to start this phase of her life that I think I simply was pulled along for the ride. I knew she was emotionally ready, intellectually more than capable, and I reminded myself as we dropped her off that first year that this was not about me but rather about her. While I knew I would miss her terribly, I was so proud of the young woman she had become that my pride and excitement for her must have overshadowed any pinches of sadness I may have felt.

Part of the difference between her leaving last year and her departure this year had to do with the packing process. Last year she was staying in the dorm; space, of course, was limited, so the packing process was much easier than this year. For her dorm life, all that was required was linen for her appointed luxurious bunk bed, her clothes, flip-flops to wear in those pleasant showers that were shared by many girls and many fungal infections, fifty-two pairs of shoes, thirty-eight pairs of earrings, 185 photos of friends and family, and of course 253 movies. Sarah is my little girl who could watch a movie 110 times and still laugh at the lines as if it were the first time she was hearing them.

This year packing took on a whole new feeling. Sarah was moving into an apartment. The moving process this year involved taking down her bed, taking out her nightstand, her TV, her clock, her pictures — and suddenly it hit me that she was really leaving in a different way. She would keep this apartment for at least the next three years and then move to another one for medical school and then her own home and then...wow, there was the sadness. This was Sarah leaving, really leaving, in a different way. She was not just spending a couple semesters in a dorm. This was different. Her empty room reminded me that it was different. So, with my heavy heart and the tears of course right under the surface, I spent the better part of the day talking myself through what was happening, distracting myself, and above all avoiding letting Sarah see my distress. I reminded myself that I'm a psychologist, for God's sake; I help other parents get through this. I can do it...and I almost did.

With the last of the packing almost complete and ready for placement in the moving truck — oh yeah, did I mention this year there was a moving truck? Last year it all fit in the bed of my husband's pickup truck, except the shoes and the movies; of course, they had to be shipped. As we were almost finished loading the truck, here it came, the hit from the blindside.

"Mom, I was thinking I need a little table for my kitchen, and I wondered if I could take Nana's table. I will take really great care of it, and it will make me feel like a part of Nana is with me." OK, well, there are some things we simply cannot prepare ourselves for, and for me this was one of them.

The table she was referring to is the old table that for all of my childhood and adult years sat in my grandmother's kitchen. It was the only piece of furniture that I wanted when she sold her home at the age of ninety and came to live with my parents. So, for the past ten years the table has been sitting in the basement of my home. This simple chrome-legged, white-marbled Formica top with faint green and peach lines stirs a memory in me every time I walk past it.

It's funny how the image of this table can evoke so many vivid memories with all the emotions that go with them. I know that there are many, many memories of good and bad things that have occurred in my life, but they have been erased or were never fully placed in my long-term memory. The scientist in me is intrigued by how and why we remember some things so vividly and others fade as the years pass.

From a clinical perspective, this can be explained by reviewing how memories are formed. Scientific evidence suggests that memories result when changes in connections or connection strength between neurons in the brain occur. For example, if two neurons are usually active together, the connection between them will be strengthened; therefore, over time, when one neuron is activated, it will produce activity in the other.

Consider that as a child your grandmother would bake bread in her kitchen and cut you warm pieces to share with her. You felt happy and content in her presence. Therefore, over time the smell of baking bread may elicit a memory of your grandmother, including a feeling of contentment (both neurons firing together). Similarly, if you had a negative, unhappy, or fearful relationship with your grandmother, the smell of baking bread may not only elicit an image of her, but also create an immediate sense of fear or sadness. In this case the smell of bread "turned on" the connection of neurons that hold a memory of fear or contentment.

When Sarah asked to take the table to college with her, it turned on the neuronal connections in my brain, and I immediately began to recall all that had occurred around that table and how I felt when I got my first apartment during college, when this table sat in my kitchen.

The table memories for me began when I was a little girl. It served as the kids table during holiday meals. Now, most of you know that the creation of a kids table for holiday meals was really just a secret plot by the adults to put the kids out of sight so they could talk and enjoy their food without interruptions. But my two sisters and my three cousins and I didn't mind eating at the table; it made us feel special. And secretly for me it was a great opportunity to hide the food I didn't want to eat, which was most everything back in those days (time and age has certainly changed that).

The table was quite small; even with the leaves fully extended, it could really only accommodate four chairs. So the six of us kids would often end up sharing chairs or squeezing extra chairs on the corners, which allowed us to elbow each other and fight over who had more space and whose plate was touching whose silverware. It was at this table that as a child I watched my father hold my cousin upside down as my uncle pulled a chicken bone from his throat during a Christmas dinner. It was the place that we kids would hide in the hopes of catching the adults swearing or fighting. We would laugh until our sides hurt when we were successful.

During the summer I would often spend weekends with my grandmother and looked forward to the lessons she would teach me at the table. I would climb up on the avocado-green chairs that sat around the table and wait for my grandmother to ask me what I wanted to do. My answer was always the same: cook. She would take out the big Tupperware bowl; even back then, its appearance was faded and worn from years of use. The noodle making process would begin with her having me count out the cups of flour and dump them in the bowl. This was followed with making a tunnel in the flour and gently placing eggs and liquid into the hole. Then I would watch as her hands would gently begin the kneading process. It always struck me how gentle she was with the dough. It was clear her hands baked with the same love and care that they showed when comforting us grandchildren when we were hurt.

She would then instruct me to put my hands into the dough. She would put her hands over mine, and we would begin the kneading process. I can recall her reminding me to put my strength into it as I folded the side of the dough together and then gently turned the ball of dough upside down in the bowl, making the sign of the cross. This was followed by covering the bowl with a pale blue blanket that she folded ever so gently to avoid any contact with the cold air on the dough. The dough would sit on that table to rise until it was time for us to punch it down, roll it out, and begin the cutting process. As I look at the size of the table today, I am still amazed that all of this activity could occur on such a small space.

The making of the noodles was then followed with the cleaning of the table and the treat that would follow. She would make us hot chocolate or chocolate milk to go with the fresh cookies that she would remove from the round yellow cookie jar. There was never a limit on the number of cookies I could have or a lecture on not making a mess. In Grandma's house and at that table, there were no rules, only love.

When I started college, working on my undergraduate degree at the University of Akron, I lived in an apartment above my grandparents' home. That is to say that I slept in the apartment but spent most of my time and ate most of my dinners with my grandparents, because despite my fierce need to be self- sufficient, I was not a fool. When the smell of fresh bread, homemade noodles, and Italian sauce made its way up the stairs, I forgot about my need for independence. While eating was truly an important part of what happened around the table, even more important was the conversation and the important "aha" moments that occurred there.

During those meals my grandfather would grill me on my study habits as we sat around the table. Education was very important to him. His parents were immigrants from Italy, and he worked most all of his childhood to help support the family. He only completed the eighth grade and then at eighteen years old went to work in the coal mines in Pennsylvania. With his limited formal education, he often spoke of feeling stupid and as a result truly valued education. I can still hear him saying, "You get your nose in those books." Now, as I am putting this sentiment to paper, it makes me laugh, but at the time I can remember frequently being frustrated.

As a matter of fact, the neuronal connections are firing and a memory is coming back to me. I can remember one time when a male friend called to tell me he was going to stop over after dinner to see me. Since I'm old it won't surprise you to know that there were no cell phones in those days. So, the call came on my apartment landline. I remember hurrying through dinner at the table in my grandparents' kitchen, running upstairs to my apartment to watch for my male visitor so I could see him coming before my grandfather did.

Although I had a separate entrance to my apartment, the front door on the porch was shared with my grandparents. That meant my guests had to cross the front porch, where my grandfather would sit in the evenings listening to the Indians games on the radio. On this particular summer evening, I had hoped he would linger a little longer at the table enjoying dessert with my grandmother. Unfortunately, that was not to be the case. I had been watching out the window, but my friend apparently was running later than expected and again without a cell phone could not let me know. So subsequently I missed seeing him pull in the driveway.

By the time I heard his motorcycle pull in and I ran down the stairs, it was too late. My grandfather already had his crooked finger in my friend's face, calling him a hippie because he rode a motorcycle and telling him he had to leave because I had my nose in the books. Of course, my young eighteen-year-old male friend left in fear and called me later to say he did not want to interfere with my studying and he was sorry. Yuck!

I cried and as usual returned to the table for words of comfort from my grandmother. She reminded me what I already knew and always felt. My grandfather, while rough in his style, always had his family's best interest at heart. It was not uncommon for me to find twenty-dollar bills in the ashtray of my car, as he always feared I would drive with my gas tank too low or would not have enough money to get food during my long days on campus. He was often gruff in his style but always quietly compassionate to those in need without ever seeking or allowing recognition.

Those four years under my grandfather's watchful eye and my grandmother's loving meals helped me to grow in knowledge and wisdom that I couldn't find in a book, no matter how far I might put my nose. Near the end of those undergraduate years, I met the amazing man who would become my husband, *and* I watched my grandfather die of cancer. The once incredibly strong-willed, proud Italian man became frail and defeated as inoperable stomach cancer slowly changed the man we all loved. Throughout those long months I would climb the stairs to my apartment, crying and wishing I could hear him fighting with my male friends and once more telling me to put my nose in the books. He no longer had the strength.

While losing a loved one in any way is painful, chronic and debilitating illnesses are particularly difficult. It is not just the final loss of the person, but watching the decline and change of their physical and emotional integrity that hurts most. My grandfather knew he was dying, but he never spoke about it and neither did the family. Instead my parents would come to the house and we would all sit at the table and talk about nothing and everything. My grandmother, who felt so out of control and lost, would make futile attempts to get him to eat, and my mother would hover around, providing as much physical care as he could tolerate. It was a painful and sad time in the house. Although very weak and only months from his death, my grandfather saw me graduate with my undergraduate degree *and* sat in the front row of the church and watched me get married. The image of the pride in his eyes still burns in the deep areas of my brain where those long-term and deeply cherished memories reside.

After we were married, my husband and I moved into my old apartment above Grandma's home while I started graduate school at Kent State University. During the final year of my doctoral program, I applied to several local hospitals and universities for my internship. However, my dream facility was Henry Ford Hospital in Detroit, Michigan. My advisors reminded me that nobody from KSU had ever been accepted for the limited positions offered at that facility and my chances were very small. My parents and grandmother were supportive, encouraging me to ignore those voices and push forward. I did. I made it to the final round of applicants and was invited for an interview, and then I waited. I recall the day the envelope arrived from Henry Ford Hospital. I opened the letter and drove to my husband's office. I had been accepted. Wow. We were so excited but now what? My accepting the offer meant I would need to move to Detroit and my husband would stay with Grandma in our apartment, as he worked in Cleveland and relocating together was not an option.

As the weeks passed and the date approached for me to give my acceptance, I began to panic. I didn't want to live apart from my husband. He of course encouraged me and reassured me that we would work out the details and that I had to accept. However, the thought of splitting the silverware, the furniture, taking my toothbrush out of the shared holder, all made me cry. I didn't want to go. I could accept my second-choice facility that made me an offer and would allow me to remain in my apartment with my husband and grandmother. What to do?

One evening while my husband was away on business, I carried the letter downstairs and Grandma and I made tea and sat at the table. While I cried she listened and then said, "Lori, this is what you have worked for the past seven years. One year will fly by regardless of whether you go or not. The difference will be that if you don't go, it will fly by *and* you will have regrets. Our purpose is often hidden in difficult decisions."

We sat at that table for hours. The decision was made. I would be starting my internship at Henry Ford Hospital in August. From a professional perspective, it was a turning point for my career.

Ironically, or as fate would have it, six months after I left, my husband was temporarily relocated to work in Indianapolis, which meant we had our apartment at Grandma's house, my apartment in Detroit, and his in Indianapolis. We traveled every weekend to see each other. The year turned out to be great professionally, and personally it became a series of honeymoon weekend experiences in three different states. What a great year — smart Grandma! I should add that prior to my husband moving to Indianapolis, he and Grandma spent six month alone, having a great time. He learned to iron his own shirts the old-fashioned way by dipping the collar and cuffs in starch. No kidding, he really did, and loved it. When I returned home, the shirts went to the dry cleaners.

He and Grandma also spent time watching Indians games and then sitting at the table dissecting every aspect of the game. It was also at that table that he enjoyed the best meals he would ever know. While every generation that has followed turned out to be great cooks, nobody can do it like Grandma. Even at one hundred years old, she still makes the best noodles and bread.

As the moving truck pulled into an apartment on the Ohio State University campus, the table was unloaded and gently placed in Sarah's kitchen in her first college apartment. Thinking about all the memories that I cherish from that table did in fact make me feel comforted and proud that the three generations of women in Sarah's life were in some way there with her.

When we arrived back home from Columbus, Nana and I sat on the couch and we began to reminisce about our years together around the table. Then the text message from Sarah arrived... "made a great dinner for Ricky and Allysa. We pulled folding chairs from the closet and put them around Nana's table...felt like home."

I shared the message with Nana, who choked back a tear and then quickly laughed and asked if Sarah's male friend rode a motorcycle. I said no and we both laughed, knowing that Grandpa would approve. When Nana Emily visits Sarah Emily in her apartment, I know they will sit at that table together, and whether they engage in deep conversation or laugh about something silly, my daughter will know the power of generational love.

7 | Fighting, Liking, and Laughing: Ingredients of Marriage and Friendships

"The best friend is likely to acquire the best wife, because a good marriage is based on the talent for friendship."

— FRIEDRICH NIETZSCHE

To love, honor, and respect all the days of our lives. The word *obey* was intentionally removed from our wedding vows. I knew marriage was nothing to be entered into lightly, so promising to do something I knew I was not capable of might start the marriage off on the wrong foot. The concept of marriage is such an interesting one. The goal is to be one, to live in harmony, to share a life. But what happens when a stubborn, high-spirited, talkative, impulsive decision-making woman who puts the toothpaste cap on halfway and never balances the checkbook marries an organized, check-balancing, toothpaste-lid closing, slow and deliberate decision-making, non-worrying kind of guy? What indeed.

Jay's first realization that perhaps he was in over his head came after the numerous times he would find himself on the floor in the middle of the night. I had never slept with anybody before and apparently my subconscious did not like the intrusion. On most nights during the first six months of marriage, I would talk loudly in my sleep (shock to nobody that knows me that I wouldn't take a break from talking even while sleeping), and then I would apparently place both of my feet on Jay's back and kick him physically out of the bed. One Sunday while having dinner at my parents, my mother looked at my bruised and exhausted new groom and suggested we may want to think about twin beds.

Jay laughed but secretly I think he was dreaming of his single life in his king-size water bed. I did feel terrible—really I did. What if I could not learn to sleep with him? This marriage stuff was harder than I thought it was going to be. Not only was I kicking the shit out of my poor husband while he was asleep and defenseless, but I also was struggling to make time to iron his shirts. I even tried simultaneously propping up books to study while ironing to save time. You know, multi-tasking. The level-headed practical husband of mine would simply suggest that we take them to the dry cleaners. But I wondered if deep down he wished I were more like Nana—if he longed for those days when she dipped his shirt collars in homemade starch and ironed them until the shirts could stand by themselves without a hanger.

Jay even expected me to enter any withdrawals that I made from the ATM machine into the checkbook. I thought this to be a bit compulsive, given that in the adding and subtracting columns of the checkbook, it still showed a balance, suggesting there was still money left. Wasn't that balanced enough? It became clear early on that separate checking accounts would help smooth over the disagreements over this compulsive balancing thing he had going. Perhaps he wasn't aware that you could simply ask the teller what your balance was when you went into the bank. Life is so much better now that there is this thing called online bill payments and electronic checking.

I admit I was young and naïve when I first got married, and I genuinely believed when you loved somebody, all the other pieces would just fall into place. I didn't expect to be so annoyed when he left socks by the couch or wanted to watch racing on TV. This was going to take some work. Perhaps I should have agreed to leave the word *obey* in the vows.

One afternoon I was sitting on the couch in our apartment studying when the phone rang. It was the landlord. He started out the call by saying, "I have received a few complaints from neighbors about the loud noises coming from your apartment at night."

I felt embarrassed. I apologized and then began to explain, "I am a restless sleeper. Sometimes I accidentally push my husband out of bed while he is sleeping. I bet the neighbors below us hear him hitting the floor. I don't do it on purpose. I am trying—"

He interrupted me and then in a quiet nervous voice said, "No, the complaint is about loud sex noises." And there it was, total humiliation. My face flushed. I felt nauseated. I quickly hung up the phone and pulled down the shades—not sure if I thought the neighbors were camped out in the bushes waiting to see my expression during the call—but I wasn't taking chances. I quickly called Jay in my fit of panic, crying and yelling, "We need to move out now. I can't live here."

In classic Jay style, he seemed to think the situation was funny and in fact seemed proud. He thought I was overreacting and tried his best to reason with me. And of course all of his reasoning tactics worked. I listened carefully to everything he said about keeping this in perspective. We were newlyweds, etc. I listened and listened and then started to pack up the apartment. We moved out one month later. Married life had begun.

Twenty-seven years later. I am thrilled to admit I stopped kicking Jay out of bed, which is a good thing because we now have a high-framed bed that is about three feet off the hardwood floor. I am happy to report that when we built our new home, we put double insulation in the walls of our bedroom and wisely purchased a five-acre piece of land so the neighbors are out of earshot.

The shirts go to the dry cleaners and we alternate taking and picking them up. I make the bed as I am the last one out of it, and Jay makes the coffee because he is the first one up. We have separate checking accounts, and I now put my socks over top of his near the couch. Neither one of us seems to care.

The rhythm of a relationship—I don't think you just fall into it. You have to work hard, fight hard, and love hard to learn it. Aging influences everything. Apparently, even our relationships are not spared the wrinkling, sagging, and at times boring routines of the passage of time. But simultaneously aging seems to carry with it a deep appreciation and understanding that it is our relationships that sustain us, nurture us, and support us when life hits us hard. There is enough research to demonstrate people who are in committed long-term relationships live longer, and suffer with less depression and despair in the later years of life. In fact we have known for years that one of the most healing and comforting things we can offer in the hospital is human connections. We require contact and connection with others to remain vibrant and well.

I don't pretend to definitively know what makes relationships work. I know that most research and experience tells us that early on in a relationship, we tend to put our best foot forward. We work hard to be polite and sensitive to each other's needs. But then years of familiarity often create opportunities to take each other for granted and to stop really seeing or hearing the other person. At a deep level we know that our most intimate relationship is the safest place to dump the frustrations and fatigue of daily life. However, over time this can create a sagging, worn-out, and rundown relationship. Sometimes we need an event, an inspirational thought, or a slap upside the head to snap us out of our complacency and realize the power of our relationships and the responsibility we have to sustain them. For me, it was medical crises and Nana's observations that got my attention.

Over the years of working with people to help them better understand and improve their relationships, and the years of living in my own marriage and sustaining my cherished friendships, I have come to believe that there are three key elements. They are learning to fight well, liking each other, and knowing how to laugh.

When couples tell me that they never fight, I soon understand why they have come in for marital counseling. It is simply not possible for two individuals with their own ideas, habits, and needs to always be in sync with each other. When there is no fighting, there is usually no communicating. No expression of needs, hurts, or wants. Eventually this leads to resentment and distance. But how can one's needs be met if they are never expressed? The lack of fighting or expressing how you feel is a problem in a marriage, but at the same time, fighting in an unfair or hurtful manner can ruin the intimacy of the marriage. Often couples will share with me that they spend a lot of time fighting over "silly things." This is because fighting over silly things like the toilet seat that was left up, the spouse who doesn't pay attention and becomes distracted during a conversation, or how the money is spent is easy. The real issue that is underneath the petty fights is where the hurt, humiliation, and anger usually reside. Learning to fight about the truth that is underneath the battle over the toilet seat or the money issues is what facilitates real intimacy and helps to maintain a relationship.

When I examine my own marriage, I have come to appreciate that fighting is a true art. It's not just about feeling entitled to say whatever you want because you feel it in the moment. The gift of aging and growing together is learning to have the patience and willingness to fight about those real issues that are underneath the fighting words. During the early years of marriage, it seemed too threatening to do this, but with age and time came the development of trust that it was safe to fight deeply about our real vulnerabilities. We have to trust that when we expose our honest thoughts to each other that they will not be used later as a weapon to cause further hurt. As it is for many couples, it is a work in progress for me as well. That said, when I was thinking about some of the most common fights Jay and I have had that I could use here, I wrote down what I thought, but decided in the spirit of collaboration that I would ask him as well. I guess I have matured.

So I texted him about what he believed our primary fights or struggles have been throughout our marriage. I was curious if my top three fight topics were the same as his. In the meantime, I asked our seventeen-year-old what she thought Dad and I fought most about. She laughed and said it's a "toss-up between racing and the fact that he gives in to Sarah and me too much." When I texted Sarah, she responded, "'Cause dad is a pushover and you feel you have to be the one setting the rules too much." She added, "No complaints about that on my end J." I raised beautiful, sweet, smart-ass girls. Then came the text response from Jay, "Aw shit… am I in trouble AGAIN?! L" And married life continues.

The truth is — the girls are right, and so is Jay. He is a pushover with them and that drives me crazy, and probably he is in trouble again for an issue yet to be uncovered. When battling about the girls, the deeper issue is I feel he wants to take the easier route to make them happy and avoid fighting, and I am left setting the boundaries and worrying, always worrying, which makes me less popular. And money is often a fight for us as I tend to be more of a saver and Jay is more willing to spend money easily. We both acknowledge that the issue under the surface of the fight is my long-term planning and control needs, and Jay's ability to live more for the moment and to spend money on enjoying life now. We work regularly to find our balance.

Since both the girls and Jay identified racing as a source of fighting, I decided to finally acknowledge it and share the tension and fear underneath that sensitive issue.

Jay is a huge fan of drag racing. He tells stories about when he was a little boy watching drag racing with his dad, about the neighbor down the street who had a hot rod that he raced and how all the kids would hang out in the garage watching him work on the car. I never understood. In fact I am often too intolerant of it even being on the television set, whether I am watching it or not.

For many years Jay would cut photos of hot rod vehicles from a drag-racing magazine and hang them on our refrigerator and fantasize about owning one. The ritual would go something like this. He would hang the picture up. I would say, "That is stupid. What would you do with a car like that? We can't afford such a silly thing." The picture would stay there for a week or so, and then I would ask him if he wanted me to throw it away or did he want to do it. One picture would be replaced by another. This went on for years.

Seven months before Jay's fortieth birthday, I was trying to decide what we could do as a family to celebrate. Nana and I were sitting at the kitchen table, and she noticed the picture on the refrigerator. She laughed and said, "Why don't you get him one of those cars?" In hindsight this is one of those times when I should have turned a deaf ear to her voice. But instead I thought about how amazing it would be to present Jay with the gift of a lifetime. The one that he longed for, dreamed about, and knew was probably never going to be something we would compromise on. The more I thought about the idea, the more I recalled that flashy, award-winning truck that he sold many years prior to buy my engagement ring. It was his turn.

I imagined him driving his hot rod to the Kmart parking lot and sitting in a lawn chair next to the car. The hood would be up, and men and some women would walk around eating hot dogs and drinking pop, and they would stop and ask him about the car. What size motor? What year? Was it an original? All the things I witnessed people doing when I "compromised" and would go to these events on occasions — rare occasions. He would really enjoy that.

The next morning I called Jay's best friend Jan. I told him Jay had a photo of a '55 Chevy hanging on the refrigerator that I wanted to buy him in the summer for his birthday. It was in Louisville, Kentucky. Jan laughed and said these cars sell in days, maybe a week at most. It definitely wouldn't still be available by August. We would need to go and look at it now. It was the middle of January in Cleveland, Ohio. I wanted it to be a surprise, but how would we pull this off?

I decided to tell Jay I was going to Cincinnati to a conference for the day. It was far enough that it would give me enough time to justify travel, plus a full day at a meeting. Now a side note should be made that I am not a fan of driving in the snow — this has even gotten worse with age. So when the weather forecaster reported that we were in for an ice storm, Jay looked at me from across the couch and said, "Well, I guess you will not be going to your conference." Now, I knew that at 3:00 a.m., Jan would be waiting for me in the parking lot of the Marriott Hotel near the freeway with a rented flatbed trailer — just in case looking turned into buying. I could not cancel now; we were in this too deep. I made more excuses and a coffee cake to take for the ride down.

Jan was waiting as planned. The weather was not looking good, but Jan assured me that the farther south we got, we would be OK. As we drove, I shared with Jan my conversation with Jer—Jer Kilmer, the man who was selling the car. Jer spoke with a deep Southern accent. He described the features of the car over the phone to me, but seemed annoyed and bothered that I was not a hot rod lover and clearly could tell that I knew little about cars. As we got closer to Kentucky, I began to imagine what Jer would be like. I laughed and told Jan that based on our phone conversations; I pictured Jer to be a short, greasy-haired, toothless, and maybe shirtless guy.

The address on the mailbox said 242, but the house didn't look big enough to hold one maybe two people, tops. We followed the narrow driveway to the back of the house as instructed. The garage, if you could call it that, had room for ten vehicles. It stood in such stark contrast to the house. Each bay area had incredibly immaculate and meticulous tool racks. The floor did not have one piece of dirt or grease visible. The temperature and lighting seemed to be set on perfect. As we got out of the car, we were greeted by a six foot four, good-looking man with a muscular build and beautifully straight, white teeth. At first I thought this could not possibly be the same guy, and then he spoke. He looked at Jan and motioned to me. "Why did you bring her? This ain't no chick car." Yep, we were in the right place. That was Jer, Jer Kilmer. Jan simply responded, "Because she has the money."

Jan began to examine the motor and the underneath body of the car, while Jer decided to make small talk with me. He looked very uncomfortable. I imagined that not many women were allowed, or for that matter wanted, to enter his garage. He looked desperate to find something to tell me about the car that he thought I might understand. He offered, "Ya know, ma'am, the radio don't work, but the dome light does." I smiled and shook his hand and said, "Well, if the dome light works, I'll take it." Jer couldn't see that just over his left shoulder, Jan was giving me the thumbs-up, which was the clever secret code we worked out so I would know if the car was worth the asking price.

As we loaded the 55 on the bed of the truck, I thought that this was not exactly the kind of car that I imagined sitting in the Kmart parking lot with the hood up. Actually, there was no hood on this car. Instead, there were a big-block engine, 900 horsepower, and blower that had a man's winter cap over it. Jer told us that the "toboggan cap should stay on to protect the blower as we drove it up north." While I certainly noticed the roll cage and the four-foot-tall tires and the parachute that came off the back, I still thought, well, this will make a nice show car. Better than any other car in the Kmart parking lot. Jay would be thrilled.

Once we got the car home, Jan and I both realized we would not be able to keep the car in storage for Jay's actual birthday, which was in August. We would have to present it to him soon. So we decided to have a surprise party in February. The remaining month of January was filled with lies and more lies. The deed and insurance information was sent to my office. Jan had to make excuses so Jay would not stop at his shop, where the car was being stored. By the end of February, Jan and I were both exhausted with all the lies and relieved that the weather broke enough for Jan to drive the car on the road to get to the party.

Jay was surprised when he entered the front door at my parent's house, and we all yelled, "Surprise!" The video recording of that day showed him mouthing, "But it's not my birthday." We told him that a friend from out of town was coming to the party, and he had asked that we watch for him in the driveway. All of our family and friends put on their coats and proceeded as instructed to the driveway—only Jan and I knew about the car. Jay was busy greeting people and feeling overwhelmed to be having a February party for his August birthday. He didn't hear the car being fired up a quarter of a mile away.

We directed his attention to the street in time for him to see and hear the '55 Chevy coming down the street with a red bow in the grate of the car. The sound of the supercharged, 900-horsepower, big-block engine made the ground shake. The same ground that Jay came close to hitting when he realized this was the car from the picture on our refrigerator that now was his. He turned to me with shock and tears on his face. He was saying, "You didn't, you didn't." But I did because Nana suggested it. It is now thirteen years since Jay received what he claims was the gift of a lifetime.

I share this story for several reasons. First, I am quite confident that nothing then or now that I could ever buy for Jay would top this gift. It was his dream. It was the surprise of a lifetime. It meant that I heard what his heart desired and I sacrificed to work and save enough money (hidden in an envelope in my sock drawer for close to a year) to give it to him. Unfortunately, it became clear that this car was not meant for the Kmart parking lot; it was designed for racing. I wasn't stupid and probably knew this all along, but wanted to believe I could convince him to just enjoy the car. Wax it. Drive it around town a bit. First cardinal rule about marriage, you *can't* change the other person. You can try to mold him through compromise, tears, and thong underwear, but the core of the person remains intact.

I wanted to support Jay as he had always done for me, but I never fully believed he would remain persistent in his desire to race the car. His friends all tried to reassure me that he would be safe, and then they would say things like, "You bought the car for him, what did you think he would do with it?" I hate and love those friends.

The first time we went to the racetrack, I tried to distract myself by doing what I knew best to do—make it a party. I dragged Nana and the rest of my family with me to the racetrack, and we set up the grill and turned the racing experience into a family cookout. The girls loved it. They would help Jay get into his flame-retardant suite, crash helmet, and racing shoes. They would stand next to him in the staging lanes until he got close to the starting line. The girls and I then would take our seats near the area where the medical transport helicopter was sitting.

I know as Jay takes his place near the starting light, he is caught up in the moment. I know that in that moment, he is savoring the smell of the racing fuel, the sound of his tires when they are smoking, and the surge of power when the light turns green. As he makes his way to the line, the crowd, my girls, my family, and even my Nana put in their earplugs and begin to clap. To the outside world it appears that I am doing the same, but on the inside I am praying, swearing at Jay for creating this anxiety for me, and wishing it was over, which I know it will be in about nine seconds. That is what it takes for the car to fly down the quarter-mile track, reaching speeds of 140 miles per hour.

I struggle to keep from throwing up. I don't think I breathe until I see him make the turn coming back from the end of the track, and all the while I'm hating that we are there doing this. My anxiety is so high, I realize that over the years I have come to resent the car and the fear that it creates for me. The girls are right when they say that this is a source of arguments for Jay and me. I am aware that I consciously struggle with the racing issue. The car costs more money to maintain when you are racing it than I could have ever imagined. The anxiety and related anger is high when I see the racing schedule on the calendar.

And of course all the while I feel ashamed because I bought this for him and he loves it. This is the part where there should be a solution and a resolution, but to date we have not been able to find a completely satisfactory one. The compromise is that I don't typically go and watch him race and he only races in three primary races a year. It's still a work in progress. The difference in the last two years is that the arguments are more genuine. Instead of making an excuse or picking a fight with him over an unrelated issue, I will admit to being crabby because I am scared. Scared something will happen to him, worried he will break something on the car that will cost a fortune. Jay is better at understanding my fear and on a few occasions has suggested that I may want to start drinking early in the morning on the days he races. The girls laugh and suggest that drinking may not be enough—that perhaps I should start smoking pot. I don't think any of them are funny—well, maybe a little.

It seems to me that the true art of fighting is to remember that when our words are in our head and only we hear them, we are in control of them. But once we say them, they are out of our control. I work hard to be sure that the words I choose when fighting are accurate and are a true reflection of how I feel and not deliberately chosen to hit at what I clearly know are Jay's vulnerabilities. Fighting fair is about respect for not only him but for me as well. And it turns out that fighting is easier when you actually like each other.

It was an unusually warm day for October. The sky was bright blue with only a few white swirling clouds that on occasion would part to reveal glimmers of the sun. Jay drove the truck up the dirt road; through the windows, rows and rows of trees holding red and yellow apples were visible. Straight ahead was the wooden shack where we would each receive our bags and then find out what row held the Honeycrisp apples we were planning to pick.

As we all exited the truck, bags for picking the apples were handed to Nana, Sarah, Katie, Jay, and I. Nana carefully hung her bag on the end of her walker. She placed her Tupperware, napkin, and her familiar old metal paring knife on the tray of the walker and started up the row. Jay grabbed an arm to support her and we were off to pick apples. At fourteen and eleven, the girls had mastered the art of fighting. Like a great debater, they could be presented with any topic, and each one could success-fully argue the opposite side. We stopped in front of a section of trees that seemed to be filled with apples. The girls each selected separate trees to begin the picking process. This seemed like a great idea. Stay far away from each other. With little effort they each climbed to the top of separate trees. Nana positioned her lawn chair near the lower branches of a tree and began to select a few for sampling.

Jay was catching the apples the girls were throwing down to him and at him to put in the bags. Although I selected a tree in a separate row, I could still hear the girls fighting over important issues, like the fact that it wasn't fair that one took a bigger bag and the apples in one tree had worms and that one was throw-ing them farther to the ground...I was becoming more annoyed with each apple I was picking. And the mothering began. "Stop fighting. You are going to fall out of the tree if you keep horsing around. You are too loud."

I was on a roll, making valid points, when suddenly I was struck in the back by an apple. I looked up, thinking it had fallen from the tree I was standing under. Then another one hit and I heard Nana laugh. I turned around, and she was shaking her head and cutting her apple with her knife. Then I saw him. Jay hiding behind her like a coward and throwing apples at me. I wanted to be mad. I turned to say something probably clever, reminding him that it wasn't funny and he could have hurt me and was he doing that to be disrespectful while I was reprimanding the girls, but I was interrupted by Nana's voice. "Run, Jay."

With that he took off running down one of the rows. Head up in the air and arms pumping, he looked ridiculous. The girls thought it was funny and so did Nana. Without a rational thought in my head, I began to climb one of the trees next to the girls, and when I had a good visual, I began to pummel Jay with apples. I then turned and started throwing them at the girls, who were yelling at first that I was hurting them; then they began laughing hysterically as they jumped down from the tree. Victory. I showed them.

Now, this would be a great story if it ended with me jumping down from the tree beaming. Unfortunately it was gym class all over. Getting out of this tree was going to require some athletic skill, and to make matters worse, my jacket got stuck on one of the branches. As I slid down, I became wedged. I would have to ask Jay for help. I pretended I didn't need his help, and he pretended he couldn't reach me to help.

As we all got into the car with our bags of apples, Nana leaned over to me and said, "You're lucky you really like Jay and he likes you." That stuck with me. It seemed like such an odd thing to say. In hindsight it occurred to me that she was particularly sensitive and in tune with the playfulness that comes when you like somebody.

I have had the good fortune to be raised by parents who are still madly in love and who like each other after fifty-nine years of marriage. My paternal grandparents' marriage was full of love, nurturing, and commitment. They also seemed to like the same things and each other. They had their shared routine. Sitting side by side in their matching chairs with their snack trays in front of them, they would eat their meals, watch their regular TV shows, and at night my grandfather would tuck my grandmother into her twin bed next to his (twin beds—maybe she used to kick him out of bed too).

Unfortunately, Nana and Gramps's marriage did not seem to contain the liking quality of a marriage. I knew they loved each other, worried about each other, and took care of each other until his death, but I never saw the liking element. They did not seem to enjoy similar things or spend a great deal of time together. The Nana I know was not the same I observed in the context of her marriage. She never seemed as lighthearted or fun when she was with Gramps.

When I first met Jay, I was unbelievably attracted to him, that kind of attraction that takes your breath away. I did what is known as falling in love. What a strange turn of a phrase. I wonder why we don't say we jumped in love, or tumbled in love, but rather we fall into love. Falling implies that it is out of our control — perhaps it is. When we talk about love, we even make a distinction when we say, "I love him, but I am not *in love* with him." We all nod as if we intuitively know what that means. But what does it mean? I think it is an easy way to distinguish between affection and passion. Being in love connotes attraction and desire, while love seems to be more about caring and compassion. Couples who love each other say things like, "I would never want anything to happen to her. He is a good person and kind man." Being in love seems to be all of that plus an intense need to be with the other person and to genuinely *like* them.

Liking somebody, I think, is the ultimate gift in a relationship. The act of liking seems deliberate, conscious, and ever in flux. Love is important, of course, but it seems static. Once you love somebody, it is what it is — but I think liking is the active, vibrant part of a relationship. At times when our marriage feels stale or routine, as all marriages can become, we try to focus our attention more on why we like each other. Sometimes this is conscious and often I'm not sure that we are even aware it is happening.

I know many people will talk about their spouse as being their best friend, but the sentiment doesn't work for me. I don't think of Jay as my friend. I think of him in a category to be named later. But that said, Nana was right I do like him. I like that every night he places one of his folded white T-shirts on my pillow for me to sleep in. I like hearing his upbeat voice when he comes through the door and he greets the dogs. I like that when I sit on the couch next to him, he will intuitively reach for my feet to rub. I like hearing how he talks to our girls with a tone of love and support. I like watching him when he interacts with our elderly friends, always with respect and dignity. I like the way he looks at me. And I really like that he enjoys watching football as much as I do and he always lets me control the remote. It seems the little; seemingly insignificant things can create the most tension *and* the most enjoyment in relationships.

While it might well be true that we put our best efforts out there early in a marriage, we are usually also more insecure, leading to the *over interpretation* of the little things and constant need of reassurance. Emotional aging seems to bring with it better clarity into the true meaning of those little things and a sharper perspective on what is at stake if we take them for granted. Laughing seems to help us keep that perspective.

Laughter brings out the best in all of us. Researchers have shown us the myriad of health benefits in laughter. We understand that laughing triggers positive feelings in others. We laugh more when we are with others, as it appears to be more of a social activity. This is probably in part due to the fact that sitting and laughing alone only serves to make us look a little crazy. It is clear that the physical activity of laughter can function as a mini workout, with a reduction in blood pressure and heart rate. You also don't have to read the science to know that we are drawn to people who laugh and who have a good sense of humor. Laughter also seems to me to be one of the great hidden secrets to a successful marriage and friendship.

Over the years of doing marital therapy, I have noticed general themes of conflict, including money, sex, and the amount of time that either party spends with friends. These are the surface issues, but often the underneath issue is about not feeling valued or important; therefore, time with friends may pose a threat.

I would argue that a life without friends not only can leave us feeling lonely and isolated but also unfulfilled. Friendships seem to fill many of our needs, which in turn allows us to be more present and emotionally available in our marriage. They aren't interchangeable but rather complementary to each other.

My friends come in all shapes, sizes, color, sexual orientations, gender, religious and cultural backgrounds, and age. Some are my most cherished close intimate friends. Some are my go-to smart collegial friends. I shop with some, vacation with some, lunch with many, and play golf with only a few (actually, only one, because she has the patience of a saint). I know which friends to turn to when I need to confide my most sacred and confidential thoughts, and which ones I can enjoy laughing and lunching with, and which ones will be the last ones guarding my back or holding my hand.

As I look at my friendships across my first fifty years of life, I notice that the deepest and closest friends I have, I developed later in life—an unexpected gift of aging. My first friend as a preschooler was Sherri; we lived next door to each other in Akron. My two memories about her include peeing behind the house together when we didn't want to interrupt our playtime by going inside to use the bathroom, and the time I bit her on the shoulder when she wouldn't share a toy with me. We lost track of each other for forty-five years (I think she was trying to hide from me after the bite). She recently requested to be my friend on Facebook just last year. Friendship over the Internet probably feels safer to her.

My next best friend was Cara when I was in grade school. She ate at my house almost every night. We had sleepovers together, and she was the one who stood up for me when I was being picked on in gym class. She was in my wedding twenty-seven years ago and then the business of life and a geographic move interfered, and we lost track of each other. I had many great friends throughout high school, but interestingly there is only one that I am still in contact with. She remains one of my dearest and most treasured mentors, friends, and colleagues. She was my high school psychology teacher, Sister Phyllis Marie. Who would have ever guessed that the only African-American nun and the only one with a sense of humor at my all girl's Catholic high school would be my lasting friend? Sister Phyllis Marie left the convent shortly after I graduated to become Dr. Deborah Plummer. After a glass of wine, and still somewhat reluctantly, Debbie will admit that the amount of energy it took to manage my "high spiritedness" (aka excessive talking and a tendency to push the rules just a bit) may have been part of the deciding factor in her departure.

In my opinion one of the greatest sentiments about friendships comes from Stephen Schwartz, who wrote the lyrics for the song "For Good" in the musical, *Wicked*. I do believe that "people come into our lives for a reason, bringing something we must learn, and we are led to those that help us most to grow if we let them and we help them in return." The diversity of my friends makes me believe they have all come into my life for a reason and continue to contribute to who I am today. There are those wise friends whom I have had the good fortune of meeting through my professional life. While I may not share dinners or personal time with them, I do value their guidance and the friendship we share over incredible business lunches.

Janet and Bev have remained two of my close confidants from graduate school despite both of them being fifteen years older than me. We have been there for each other through breast cancer, the death of parents, and the joy of welcoming babies and grandbabies. They have both taught me about aging with beauty, honesty, and commitment to family and to friends. Despite the fact that we are all three at different points in our lives, they remain diligent and committed to making and taking time for our friendship. And the bonus is they make me laugh.

I have a handful of what Nana calls my refrigerator friends. These are the friends who feel comfortable going into my refrigerator and helping themselves to whatever they need or want, whether I am home or not. This for me is one of the greatest compliments of having familiarity and comfort with each other. A few of my refrigerator friends are only seventeen and eighteen years old — friends of my daughters who are comfortable enough to stop at our house after school to help themselves to leftovers. My friend Irene is one of the older refrigerator friends — closer to my age. Despite my resentment over her being a few years younger and having a much flatter stomach than mine, our families vacation together in a seamless way. Our two shared families have the "liking" quality of a lasting relationship. We genuinely enjoy one another's company and hold deep affection for one another. My dear friend Andrea, a beautiful and talented television personality, has been my loyal friend and professional champion. She has graciously shared the camera, her media knowledge, and her professional guidance with me for more than twenty years. Her grace and style consistently inspires me.

I just celebrated by twenty-fourth friendship anniversary with my dear friends Anita and Lori. Anita and I met when I started my first job at the VA hospital. She is a strikingly beautiful Indian woman, both inside and out. While we live on opposites sides of Cleveland (east and west, which in Cleveland is considered two different sides of the world — each of us cross the bridge to the other side with great trepidation), we commit to maintaining our friendship.

It takes work, but it has built a relationship that I am certain will still be intact when we are really old women. I know this because we have held enough trust in each other to honestly fight and hold each other accountable when necessary. We intuitively know we are there for each other. I knew she would be waiting for me in my office when I returned from having a medical procedure. Just as she knew I would be on my way before I hung up the phone after the terrible news came that her husband had suddenly and tragically died.

Lori, or the other Dr. Lori, has been my dear friend and colleague for the past twenty-four years. We met at Henry Ford Hospital during our internship year, and then thirteen years ago she had the good sense to move to Ohio and join my practice. We are both Dr. Lori. We share the same work ethic and passion for being psychologists, and are told that we look alike; but Lori definitely has a more laidback approach to life. She teaches me daily about how to worry less and stay more present focused. She also reminds me that the Clorox wipes don't need to be used daily on the doorknobs of the office.

What do you get when you have a female CEO, a female CFO, and a female director of human resources for a major hospital introduced to a female psychologist? The prettiest, prettiest club. That's right, six years ago I was enriched when three other incredible women came into my life. Susan, Becky and Danielle are certainly an eclectic group of women; on the surface one would not have predicted a deep and lasting friendship could have developed. Many would never imagine us having anything in common. We range in age from sixty-one to forty. One has grandchildren, one is pregnant, one is gay, and one likes Paul Anka and Tom Jones. And collectively we find one another to be the prettiest human beings we have ever known. We have dinner together once a month. They challenge me and push me to be smarter, stronger, and prettier than I really am. They set the bar high and then lower it just enough so I can succeed.

Nana tells me that her opportunities for meeting friends were limited. She spent a lot of time with her siblings and the neighbor women because they were close in geography and therefore easy to maintain. They were all similar—same age, all Christian, all white, and all raising children, while cooking and taking care of their homes. She thinks the diversity of my friends is a unique treasure. I agree.

Early in my life my friendships were formed from convenience, proximity, and shared interests and beliefs. With age and time pressures, I think we become more selective about our friends. We choose wisely. It seems that with maturity, we are drawn to people who can still teach us those missing life lessons—the ones who help us fully realize our potential. If you removed even one of my friendships, I would somehow be different. While Nana's voice is clearly the loudest in my head, it is complemented by the brilliant thoughts and words of my very different friends.

Each of these incredible women has woven her own piece into the creation of who I am today. Friendships take time energy and commitment, which I appreciate are often scarce resources in our busy lives. But the return on investment can be life altering and life sustaining. The true appreciation of this fact has come to me with age. While there are many uncertainties in life, I know with confidence that whether I am standing in the center of a room at a party or in the front of a funeral home, my friends will be walking through the door.

8 | *Bowel Movements: Keeping Life Moving*

"There is some good in the worst of us and some evil in the best of us. When we discover this, we are less prone to hate our enemies."

— Martin Luther King, Jr.

Poop. I can't seem to get away from the chatter about poop. Last week I left my office got in the car and started my drive home when I passed a sign for a health spa that was offering colonic cleanses, which is the fashionable way of saying you are going to get an enema followed by diarrhea. Cleansing your colon or detoxifying your body of toxins seems to be in vogue these days. It's talked about in every fashion magazine, on the news, and occasionally discussed by the medical community. Everybody who is anybody is doing it. I thought perhaps I should call up my friends and suggest that after our weekly girl's lunch meeting, we could go to have our eyebrows tweezed, get a pedicure, and then have our colons flushed free of poop. Now, that could be a great girl's day out.

As I continued to drive, I started to wonder, "When did our colons get dirty?" What seems to be this new obsession with bowel movements for younger adults? I know that for as long as I have worked in the field of geriatrics, I have consistently heard *seniors* lament about their bowel movements. Did they have one?

Should they worry if they don't go for two days? Do they need to go twice a day for good health? Should they be drinking more fruit juices? And then there is the conversation about color and consistency. Over the years I have become immune to these conversations. I expect and anticipate that if a patient is over the age of seventy, no matter what we are discussing, the conversation will eventually turn to bowel movements.

"How was your vacation, Mrs. Jones?" Beautiful weather, but the food left me constipated. "Mr. Smith, how did your visit with your family go?" I was so nervous, I had diarrhea for the first few days and I was afraid to leave the house."

While I seem to be comfortable with these conversations — not sure what that says about me — I know that for many caregivers these bowel conversations can be incredibly frustrating and stressful. In fact, I recall a conversation I had with my mother the other day when she was voicing her frustration about my grandmother, who has suddenly started to focus on and worry about her bowels. Fortunately, Grandma didn't start this obsession until she was approaching one hundred years old. But it drives my mother crazy.

Ironically, it was a bowel obstruction just six months ago that almost took my grandmother's life. I stood over her while the doctor tried to put a nasogastric tube down through her nose, past her throat, down the esophagus, and into her stomach. The tube was necessary to aspirate gastric secretions from her stomach to reduce her pain and to avoid potential complications while we waited for the obstruction to correct. The procedure was painful. She was crying and uncomfortable, and unable to swallow the tube. The tube would pass through the nose but end up wadded in her mouth instead of going down her esophagus into her stomach.

"No more," she was crying. My parents and husband began to cry and stepped out of the room. I held her arms down and looked into those blue eyes and said, "Listen to my voice. When I say swallow, you need to swallow." The next pass was unsuccessful again, but the third time I yelled in my raspy voice, her voice, "Swallow!" The tube passed. With the tube in place, she began to experience some relief from her pain. By the evening, she was back to her usual funny, engaging self, despite the potential seriousness of the condition.

One young nurse entered the room and in a booming loud voice yelled, "Hi, sweetie, Can you tell me when you pooped last?" I was so annoyed, thinking to myself she obviously saw my grandmother's age and assumed she was probably hard of hearing and perhaps demented. I hate when people assume that the elderly like to be called by the same words of endearment that we use for children and small animals. Do they do this because it makes them feel that they have shifted the power differential or because they simply do not know how to address our elderly with the dignity they have so clearly earned over their lifetime? How does Dr. Smith at the age of eighty suddenly become "honey"? Or how does Mrs. Smith suddenly earn the title of "sweetie"? Yuck. And really, you are a professional saying the word "poop" to my grandmother?

As I continued my internal angry rant, I looked over at my grandmother. She was smiling and responded, "I had my last bowel movement two days ago. I am here because I have a bowel obstruction." The nurse blinked and apologized, as she did not realize that was why Nana was in the hospital. Nana and I started to laugh so hard that we did not hear the doctor come into the room.

Dr. Noall took a different approach, her usual respectful and playful approach with Nana. "Mrs. Serian—"

"Emily," Nana corrected her.

"Emily, we need to begin to discuss what we will do if this obstruction does not correct itself." She went on to explain that at Nana's age, she was not a candidate for surgery. She began to systematically discuss Nana's end-of-life decisions. "If your heart stops, do you want us to…would you want a feeding tube placed if…what do want us to do if…"

Without fear or hesitation, Nana laid out her wishes. I felt sick. The seriousness of our poop dilemma was beginning to sink into my awareness. As I slept in the chair next to her hospital bed that night, I thought how ironic that the years of joking about our bowels no longer seemed funny. With all that Nana had lived through, her complicated medial conditions during her first fifty years of life, followed by the many losses and emotional challenges during her second fifty years, it could all end because of her inability to poop — to keep life moving.

She looked content and happy as she slept. It was the ending that we all prayed would be hers. We hoped she would be free of pain and suffering and would simply drift off in her sleep. How practical and mature. But now faced with the reality, I decided to hell with that. I was not ready. I whispered in her ear, "I am telling you, old lady, you better poop tomorrow." With her eyes still closed she responded, "You're the boss."

For the next several days, family members called and Skyped, to check on the status of her bowels. Our conversations alternated between humor and fear. Nana provided the humor. She laughed and said, "I told you my bowels were important." This was the one and only time that we all agreed that talking about her poop was a good thing. The daily conversations with the staff included a focus on the presence or absences of bowel sounds and queries about whether or not she felt like she could poop. Then after our third walk up and down the hall, it happened. The family texting chain began. *Nana will live. She pooped.*

Medically, most care professionals would argue that if we take good care of ourselves — eat right, exercise, and manage stress in our lives — our digestive system naturally will eliminate toxins and waste and will continue to move in a normal rhythm. Ah, the key, we must take good care of ourselves to allow our body to keep things moving naturally. Who knew that a great metaphor for life could be found in our colon? Maybe this is why during those times in our life when we feel most out of control and stuck, like with aging, we begin to focus and obsess on our bowels. Or when we are holding on to toxic thoughts or relationships, we feel compelled to cleanse and detoxify.

Over the years of doing therapy, I have been inspired by the power of forgiveness in helping people move forward in life. Forgiveness has the power to release people from toxic experiences and free them to more fully live life. The story of Mr. C brings to life everything that the research shows us, which is that the act of forgiving is one of the most powerful healing tools for our health. It is a life-altering experience that keeps us moving forward, but it is often the most difficult.

About five year ago, I was listening to my messages in the office. I pressed the button on our recorder to retrieve them and began to write down phone numbers and messages. After twenty-some years, I can usually anticipate what the caller will say. Need an appointment for treatment of depression, anxiety, divorce, medical illness, job loss, etc.

But every so often there is a call that makes me feel like I have been punched in the stomach. This was one of them. The quiet voice of a man fighting back tears came on the machine. "My twenty-eight-year-old daughter was killed in Iraq. I need some help."

Mr. C came into my office and sat low on the couch. The heaviness of his burden could be felt and observed in the way his body sank into the sofa. He looked at me and before I could ask my first question, he took off his glasses and began to sob. The crying was deep and hard. Then the words, "I was teaching my fourth-grade gym class and the principal called me to come to the office. When I walked into the reception area, my heart started to beat fast. I knew something was wrong. 'There is a phone call for you.' The voice on the other end of the phone cried and told me that my daughter was dead. My daughter was a civilian on a peacekeeping mission in Iraq, and her convoy was targeted in an act of terrorism. She was a beautiful blond American—perfect for a kidnapping they said. But no, she was more–she was *my* beautiful daughter and they killed her. They riddled her car with bullets and then tossed a grenade under her car. They killed her. She's dead. She burned to death." His gaze was empty.

Over the first several years, the anger burned inside of him. He blamed God for not doing what God was supposed to do... save her. He blamed himself for not being the father who protected her, or the one who forbid her to go, and for being the father who hadn't told her enough that he loved her. He raged at our government and the security company who had sent her that day into a dangerous area. Why had they not known better? What was the government hiding in the "classified" file? Then of course the anger turned to those who had set the bomb and killed her. He fantasized about retaliation.

The deep seeds of anger gave way to total despair and loss. He reminisced about her days as a little girl, when they would walk to school together, and he would teach her in gym class. Raw pain revealed itself one day when he stumbled on her baseball mitt in the garage. For months he would hold it, smell it, and play old images in his head of her playing catch with him in the front yard and playing for her high school team. He sobbed with the memory. Then looked up and asked, "Do your daughters play softball?" His question hit me hard. It was unexpected. The answer would bring a deeper connection between the two of us. It forced my mind to relate to his words in a personal way. Yes, I had daughters who played softball. Yes, their mitts were sitting on a shelf in the garage. A quick flash of an image of losing them as he lost his daughter forced me to take a long deep breath to maintain composure before answering his question.

Empathy is a powerful component of therapy. It is the ability to identify with another person's feelings — to emotionally put yourself in their shoes by understanding and identifying your own feelings. Oftentimes empathizing makes us vulnerable to our own fears and pain. This was one of those times. I would have loved to have shifted the topic away to another area, off of me, off of making the connection with my daughters and the unbearable thought of ever losing them as Mr.C had lost his.

"Yes I do", I answered. He smiled through his tears. "I hope you remind them to play for the enjoyment of the game." I nodded. I thought about how many times I heard Nana tell the girls to "Play hard but never forget to have fun. It's only a game."

Mr. C's pain and sorrow would intensify when he reflected on the things that most fathers imagine — like walking their daughter's down the aisle. Andi was engaged to be married when she died. It was the ending of a father's dream. He would not walk her down the aisle. He would not see her children. He would not be able to tell her how much he loved her. Most days the sadness and pain was unbearable. He remained stuck in alternating despair and anger for the better part of three years. His soul would carry a scar forever and nothing would change that, but one day we began to explore the concept of forgiveness.

I reminded him that forgiveness does not justify the wrong that has been done or take away the responsibility of the person who created or caused the pain. In fact forgiveness really has little to do with the person who hurt us. It is a gift we give to ourselves. It is our decision to let go of feelings of resentment and revenge that weigh heavy on us and hold us back from experiencing peace and happiness. It is important in trying to keep moving forward with our life and to not become stuck or bound up with toxic thoughts of resentment.

Slowly Mr. C began to digest the concept that perhaps he needed to let go of his anger and find a way to forgive — not forgive the act that took her life, but forgive himself for what he believed were his inadequacies that led to her death. He began to write in journals about his grief. He wrote poetry about his experience. He and his family set up a foundation in his daughter's memory, and he began to actively engage in fund-raising and speaking events. Forgiving himself did not come easy or completely. At this, the five-year anniversary of his daughter's death, he still hangs on to regrets that fuel his pain, but in those moments when he lets go and embraces forgiveness, he admits to feeling closer to her and at peace. He has not moved on, but he has moved forward with his life.

As a psychologist for over twenty years, I have had the privilege of working with many people through their most painful struggles, life's obstacles, and sometimes great tragedies. I have continued to be amazed by the resilience, strength, and integrity of the human spirit to cope and at times thrive through adversity. Through it all the common thread of moving forward in life seems to come from forgiveness and gratitude.

I am consistently inspired by people who can embrace the art of forgiveness so comfortably. I on the other hand have to consciously and mindfully work to let go of a hurt. The grudge is so easily fueled by the voice in our head that reminds us we are justified in being angry and not forgiving, because after all, what was done to us was not right. It is important to be right, isn't it?

My grandmother always says that carrying a grudge is exhausting. She is right, of course. When I am stubborn and hold on so tight to my hurt or anger, I am physically and mentally exhausted. Forgiving and letting go of the hurt is so freeing and keeps me moving. As I age and begin to reflect on the remaining years of my life, it has become clearer to me that holding on to resentments robs me and only me of enjoying great moments, experiencing peaceful days, and embracing incredible experiences.

9 | The Moment: When the Other Shoe Drops

"And in the end, it is not the years in your life that count. It's the life in your years."

— ABRAHAM LINCOLN

The sun was beginning to drop in the sky, creating soft colors to the horizon. It had been yet another picture-perfect day on the shores of Sanibel Island, Florida. The spring break trip to Sanibel began when Sarah was just a year old, and we have returned every year together as a family. Vacations are such an important and valued tradition for our family. We love the dedicated time it affords us to be together—some of our best family conversations and laughs happen during those times, without all the other distractions of our lives. However, our family was getting older and changes had begun. This was our first trip without Sarah. The spring break schedules for Katie's high school and Sarah's college did not match up. It was to be another great trip but different.

Katie was taking a late-afternoon swim while Jay and I decided to play tennis. That is to say that Jay would serve the ball to me and I would hit it back to him off the court and near the alligator pond. After the third consecutive time he had to retrieve the ball from the swamp area, he began to complain that the back

91

half of his leg was hurting. He blamed it on his tennis shoes, and I blamed it on the fact that he had to climb down the hill toward the pond so many times to retrieve tennis balls. I mean, really, who puts a tennis court near an alligator pond.

The next day we decided to skip tennis to avoid the leg cramping, and Jay spent the day in his flip-flop shoes, mostly sitting at the beach as this was our last day of vacation.

As we exited the airport, the sun was shining and the air was unusually warm for late April in Cleveland. The three of us climbed on the airport shuttle bus to get to our car. As Jay took the last step up, he felt that tight cramping feeling again. We laughed at what a great tennis player I am, that I really gave him a workout.

By the time we pulled in our driveway, it was really late, with an early start in the morning for all of us. So the suitcases were left in the laundry room with the promise that after work the sorting process would begin. I climbed into bed; the sheets felt crisp and clean, and the pillow felt right, familiar and comfortable. I moved in closer to Jay and felt for his hand, which I knew would be resting half under his pillow, waiting for me to hold it as I usually do just before I fall asleep.

I wondered why my bed always feels so much better when I have been away from it for a while. Is it that I forget how comfortable it is when I am in it every night? Does the time spent in an unfamiliar bed that doesn't really fit my body the same give me perspective and appreciation for what is familiar and comforting? The sound of Katie upstairs climbing into bed distracted me from my thoughts. The house was quiet. I had texted Sarah earlier to let her know we were home, but I reminded myself to call her in the morning. With that thought I fell asleep, a deep comfortable happy sleep.

The morning was filled with the usual sounds and smells. Coffee brewing, dogs running around, Katie's hairdryer going, and the *Today* show playing in the bedroom—the usual start to a day. One by one we left the house. Jay yelled up the steps his good-bye to Katie, "Bye, sweetie pie. Have a good day." He kissed me good-bye with the usual phrase, "I love you. Have a good day. I will see you back here in the nest." For many years, we have referred to our bed as the nest. It is the place we come back to every night to snuggle in, feel safe, warm, and connected to each other. The nest—it never occurred to either of us that maybe we would not be returning to the nest. Katie ran down the steps, kissed me good-bye, grabbed her lunch, and left for school. I grabbed my coffee and left for the hospital for our senior assessment clinic. The first patient was scheduled at 8:00 a.m. I would have just enough time to check a few e-mails. The vacation was officially over and the routine had begun.

At 10:40 a.m., study hall time, I got a text from Katie that she had forgotten her money for an afterschool event. Could I drop it off at lunchtime? With Katie, this seemed to happen so often that being annoyed was a waste of energy. I quickly texted, "OK." The next patient was brought into the room and I pushed on with the day. At about 11:45 a.m. my phone rang. Typically I would not answer, but I saw Jay's work number appear on the screen. He normally called from his cell phone. When I picked up the phone, the sound in his voice made my heart start to beat faster. "I am sitting here at my desk, and I am having horrible, stabbing chest pain. I can breathe, and I am not short of breath, but I think I need to get to a hospital to be sure."

The moment. The time when nothing seems familiar, nothing is routine and mundane, and nothing is logical, including my thoughts. Why didn't I yell, "Call 911!" It is exactly what I would have said to a friend, to a patient, to my parents, but not to Jay. The voices in my head started. No, this can't be serious. He is healthy. He is in great physical shape. He exercises and eats better than most people I know. Let's not panic. Oh my God, I need to be with him. It will take me forty-five minutes to get there. I am on staff at one of the closest hospitals to his facility, but I don't trust them. I don't want him to go there. If it is serious, I need to get him downtown. How will I get him downtown? Maybe this is just a muscle pull.

I finally speak. "OK, babe, do you feel like you need to go to the hospital? Or do you want to go to the urgent care and I will meet you there?"

"No, don't leave work," he said. "The pain is getting better. I think I may have pulled a muscle. I will drive over to the urgent care to have it checked.

"I am on my way anyway," I responded. "I love you. See you soon." I rarely say "see you soon." Why hadn't I said good-bye, which is typical and usual?

I grabbed my purse. I asked the receptionist to apologize to the family and the patient and please reschedule them. The car ride there seemed to take forever. I pulled into the parking area and saw his truck. Just seeing his truck made me feel better — good, he was here and everything would be fine. When I entered the waiting area, the staff recognized me and motioned me to come back to the exam room. There he was, lying on the table with no shirt on, looking sexy, tan, and handsome with a smile on his face. What a relief, he was fine. The doctor was finishing his exam and completing the history about the sudden pain that Jay had experienced, which was now significantly better. Jay shared with him that we just gotten back from vacation and that while there he did have some cramping in his leg. But it was not red or swollen, leading us not to be concerned.

Tennis — we were playing tennis when I first felt the pain, Jay added. Then he smiled at me. OK, I came clean. I piped in and admitted that we weren't really playing tennis, but rather I was hitting balls and Jay was retrieving them from the mouths of alligators. We all laughed. What a relief. How lucky we were that this wasn't something serious.

The doctor suggested we head over to the emergency room to have a CT scan of the area just to be on the safe side. We agreed, but my thoughts had already turned to the remaining schedule of the day. I would call the office while I was waiting in the ER and then stop at the grocery store on the way home. Maybe I would get thin pork chops that I could make quickly, as I was sure the CT process would take a couple hours. Perhaps I would take my laptop in to get some work done while we waited.

When we arrived at the ER, Jay was taken down for his scan; he was having some pain that intermittently was quite intense. It certainly seemed to be a bad muscle pull. He was grimacing in pain. I approached the side of his bed and asked if I could get him anything. He simultaneously winced in pain and smiled, then suggested that sex might help. I laughed and he tried to laugh, but his ribs hurt too much.

We turned our conversation to what to do about food. Should we pick something up on our way home, or should I make something? Our conversation was interrupted by a heavyset doctor who entered the room but kept his eyes focused on his shoes. With one seemingly simply and easy sentence he said, "You have a pulmonary embolus. We are going to take you up to ICU." And with that he pulled the curtain back and left.

Jay stared at me and I felt compelled to "hurry." Adrenaline was surging through my body. I wanted to run. I knew just enough about medicine to realize that we were in danger. I just didn't fully appreciate how grave the danger was. I ran into the bathroom of the emergency room that Jay was in and called a friend of mine, who is a pulmonologist at the hospital. He heard my voice and the words "pulmonary embolus." He was not on call but told me he would be there in fifteen minutes.

I went back to the side of the gurney and looked down at Jay, willing myself not to cry. I couldn't scare him. He was going to be fine. He looked great. As they prepared to take him upstairs, the pulmonologist arrived. They began to wheel Jay down the hall. I was asked to follow the pulmonologist to the back corner of the nursing station to a computer screen. Typically there would be some small talk between us, as we have known each other for more than twenty years. There was no chatter. He motioned for me to sit in the chair next to him. I looked into his eyes and felt my body grow increasingly hot. I was aware of the beads of sweat dripping down my back.

With a soft and slow voice, he said, "Lori, this is serious. Do you see this area?" He pointed to the computer, which revealed a cross-sectional view of Jay's lung. Dr. Kaplan was pointing to an area on the image. He went on, "This is one of the largest pulmonary clots that I have seen in somebody who has survived. The only area that allowed blood to flow and kept Jay alive was smaller than the diameter of a strand of hair."

He went on to point to each of the lobes of the lungs. "The clot hit here and then broke into these eight clots we see in the right lobe and the seven you see in the left." When he broke his gaze from the computer and looked at me, I saw it in his eyes. The fear flooded over me, and I knew in that moment that what was normal and familiar would forever be different. We were not going back to the nest tonight.

Once Jay was in his room, they gave him an injection of a blood thinner to minimize the risk of another clot. The next several days would be high risk for another clot until the blood could become thinner with medications. The existing clots that were still causing him pain would ultimately dissolve, but could take up to three months.

While I lay in the chair next to his bed watching him sleep off and on, I thought, how could we have ever seen this coming? I thought about how we laughed about his leg pain when we were playing tennis just a few days ago—forever ago. Yet, it was that very pain that was the signal that he had a clot forming in his leg. It was nothing. It was a "shake it off, we are getting old" complaint. We didn't see this shoe dropping. It was not a symptom of an aging, out-of-shape, tennis-playing body. It was a clot that would ultimately travel to his lungs, creating the intense pain he reported when he was sitting at his desk. It was a clot that almost took his life.

We now appreciate that was the moment when the clot might have hit a different way or might not have passed through the pulmonary vein. He would have died in an instant. There would have been no conversation about whether or not to go to the walk-in clinic or call the emergency room. The last words I would have ever heard from him would have been, "I'll see you back here in the nest."

Jay woke up at about 3:00 a.m. with pain starting in his other leg. We tried walking the halls to keep blood flowing. But the panic began to rise up in both of us. We walked and sobbed and both felt so helpless and scared. What if this was another clot? The on-call doctor was notified. We waited. We became paralyzed by what was happening. Jay cried and began to talk about his fear of dying.

"I don't want to die. I want to walk my girls down the aisle on their wedding day. I don't want to leave you alone—alone to raise our girls, to grow old without me here to take care of you. I don't want you to reach under the pillow for my hand and not find it there." I could not bear the pain or the fear that was rising up in me. I felt like I was exploding on the inside. I wanted so desperately to turn the clock back to that moment before I fell asleep last night. Where was the warning? Our lives were flowing, moving; things were orderly and predictable. We hustled out of the house in the morning without a warning that this was the day our lives would be changed.

For the first time in my life I fully and completely understood the meaning of no control. It's ironic that we spend most of our life worrying about, "What if…," as if somehow that worry about something unknown prepares us for the real life-changing moment. It doesn't. In fact, most of what we worry about are the things we *can* anticipate or fear, which usually never happen. It's the hit from the blindside — the other shoe that drops that we never see coming — that is worth our worry.

I struggled the better part of that night to catch my breath, knowing that in the morning I would need to make the painful phone calls. Katie knew Jay had been admitted to the hospital, but we chose to hold off on the details until morning when we were prepared to answer questions. She spoke to Jay when he got settled into his room to say good night. We had called Sarah at school to tell her the truth about the clot, but again details and questions would be better answered in the morning, including whether she should come home, which was a five-hour drive.

I had called my parents but asked them not to wake Nana to tell her what had happened. I knew how devastating this would be for her, and I could not risk something happening to her in the middle of it all. But I knew I was just borrowing time. Jay's parents had both passed away more than ten years earlier. I would not need to call them. The fleeting thought of them being gone left me feeling overwhelmed and alone. He didn't have parents to take care of him or to be here with me. How strange that I would think about that for a fifty-three-year-old man. I guess age doesn't matter when we slip into our roles as parents and children. But I was keenly aware in that moment that the girls and I were his only family. An intense need to protect him flooded over me.

Throughout the night the frequent blood draws continued to check on the progress of the thinning of his blood. In addition, tests were run to try to discern what caused such a clot in a healthy man. By the time the sun was coming up, my phone started to ring. Jay's boss had called to offer to have a medical helicopter transport Jay downtown for specialized care. They offered support to me for anything I needed. It became clear that the girls needed to be here at the hospital with us. They needed to see Jay. I knew they wanted our normal life back. I could hear the pain and fear in each of their voices. They were reassuring me and themselves that Dad would be OK. He had to be.

It was time for the call to Nana. I knew before I hit the Send button on the phone what her words would be to Jay and what she would say to me. I heard the voice in my head. She spoke to Jay first, who mustered every bit of energy to appear upbeat and well on the phone.

"Hey, lady, I missed the game last night. How did our Indians do?" They chatted for a while, with laughing and crying on both ends of the phone. Then he handed the phone to me. When I heard her voice, I started to cry. She cried. She expressed worry and concern for me.

And then she said, "This is your blessing, a reminder of how precious every moment of life is…don't forget."

How could I? I never would again. I vowed to remember this feeling of gratitude as I looked at Jay smiling in the hospital bed, looking at me. This moment would be seared in my brain.

The first anniversary of this horrible moment came and went without any outward recognition by any of us. But I know that looking at the last year; the moment changed all of us. Life still moves as it did, but we are all more aware. We are all more fragile—breakable. Despite our efforts to return the house to normal, the girls are keenly aware of times when Jay looks tired or is taking an unusual nap on the couch. The girls will frequently ask if Dad's OK. The tone of their voice and the way they look at me when they ask reminds me that they still feel vulnerable.

We were changed by that moment. There isn't a day that goes by that we don't leave the house in the morning without kissing each other good-bye. The poster board in Katie's room now has inspirational sayings about gratitude written on it, and Sarah texts Jay more often than she did in the past. The mixed blessing is that our family walks around still wounded by what occurred and what could have been, but we also have entered into a place of mindful gratitude. Admittedly, I still have moments where fear of losing Jay creeps in, but I try to replace them with thoughts that I have him today. As a family, we consciously live by Nana's philosophy of treating each day as a gift. The horrible moment at roughly 11:30 a.m. on a beautiful April day changed our sense of security but also snapped us out of complacency. We no longer take things for granted in the way we did before that day. We have been changed forever.

10 | *The Game of Baseball: It's All About Our Perspective*

"Every strike brings me closer to the next home run."

— BABE RUTH

W hen I was in grade school, I hated gym class. The whole process created great anxiety for me. First, there were the changing areas that the girls and boys were separated into to prepare for class. The boys would stay in the classroom, and the girls would go into the bathroom to quickly put on our tennis shoes, baggy shorts, and floppy white tops. There was never enough room for everybody in the bathroom, there was no privacy (not that seeing one another's training bras was a big deal, but the fact that we had no choice created tension), and then there was hair. We were expected to have it pulled back in a ponytail with no loose strands. This all was to be accomplished while Sister Ann stood by the door hurrying us along.

Once we got into the gym, the real fun would begin. We would all line up against the cinder-block wall that always felt cold even on hot days. The gym floor always felt sticky with a combined odor of dirty feet and glue. Just standing there made me nervous. Sister Ann was always quite a vision with her habit covering everything but her round face just below her eyebrows. She wore her usual black dress and huge silver, scary cross around her neck, but on gym days she added a whistle to her neck apparel and traded in her black shoes for white tennis shoes.

She would enter the gym with a quick pace as if she were warming up for a sprint or marathon or some kind of athletic thing that I did not pretend to understand. Once she reached the wall where we were all lined up, she would select two people to be the team captains. I was never selected. The team captains were always the star athletes of our class. Then systematically the captains would select their team. "I pick Joe, I pick Tina, I pick Sam, I pick Donna, I pick Cara, I pick Jason"…this went on until we all were on a team. Jack and I were always the last ones to be selected. Jack wore dirty clothes and always smelled like he had just cleaned a horse stall. He had no friends and most of the class never wanted to stand by him. I felt sorry for Jack and at times I would offer him gum, hoping that some of the smell would be concealed and maybe one of the other boys would eat with him at lunch.

I was picked last because no matter how hard I practiced, I could never kick the ball, hit the ball, shoot the ball, or run without my legs turning out, making me look like a bird running with two broken wings. I wanted so bad to be cool like Tina. She was great at all the games and looked so pretty even when she was sweating. Sister Ann used to tell me that I just didn't concentrate enough and that when we do our part and try, God would find a way to help us accomplish what we truly wanted. I really wanted to believe her, but mostly I wanted to kick the ball and get on first base just once.

Kickball was usually the game we played on nice days. I hated nice days. "Lori, you're up." Joe and Jason would moan, "Why can't somebody else take her turn?" Then Sam and Donna would begin the chant, "Easy out, easy out." Although I would pray all the while the ball was rolled to me, I would usually either kick too late, making my foot go over the top of the ball, or kick too soon so the ball would simply be tipped from my foot, allowing me to begin my bird run of only five or six steps before the ball would hit me out. I used to think even God knows I will never kick that ball, never make it to first base.

Why was it so hard for me to have coordination in my feet? My parents took me to see a specialist when the lack of coordination turned to pain in my legs. The medical opinion back then was that it was an orthopedic abnormality, which ultimately led to surgery on both of my feet to relax the very high arches, followed by six months of wearing casts on my legs. Not a pleasant experience, and the surgery did not make a difference, but it did get me out of gym class for all of seventh grade. It was worth it.

However, the real answer for why I couldn't kick that ball came just last year when I saw a neurologist for migraine headaches. She completed a neurological exam, asking me to squeeze her hands and stick out my tongue, and then she took a pin and began pricking my feet. I could see her doing it, but I wasn't really feeling it. She looked at me and I knew something was not right. She asked about my feet and my surgery. It turned out that what was described as an orthopedic issue when I was young was a condition known as Charcot-Marie-Tooth disease, which is known as a hereditary motor and sensory neuropathy. It is a group of hereditary disorders that affects the nerves in your arms and legs. The disease predominantly causes muscle weakness, poor coordination, frequent falls, and limited sensations in the feet as the nerves progressively die.

As I sat on the exam table, I engaged in an intellectual conversation, but the room felt hot and my thoughts kept returning to the word *hereditary*. I was always aware that my girls had the same "weird feet," with my high arches and curved toes, but it was not a point of concern until now. Katelyn had a somewhat elevated arch, but Sarah's feet were identical in appearance to mine. Please, not another condition for Sarah to have to face.

The flashback began. When Sarah was in preschool, we signed her up for a T-ball team. My husband, Jay, was one of her coaches, so he was always on the field working with her and providing encouragement and direction to all the children. I had the view from a blanket in the grass. I would watch her hit that ball off that T with great pride, but when it came time for her to run to first base, I recall that all-too-familiar knot forming in my stomach. Why did she seem to have so much trouble running? Push that thought away, push it away. Sarah was not

103

feeling ostracized by her team or her coaches; she was having fun. Ignore the knot. Ignore it.

When Sarah started first grade, one day she came home from school and shared with me that she didn't like gym class because her legs would get tired and would hurt. The alarm inside started to sound again. I took her to her pediatrician, who told me I was over reacting and should not worry. So of course I took that to heart, came home, and had a good night's sleep. Really? No, I came home and called the office of Dr. Thompson, the chief of pediatric orthopedics at Rainbow Babies and Children's Hospital in Cleveland, Ohio. We had an appointment to see his colleague the following Thursday. How do I know that? I guess it is the way we know what we were doing the morning of 9/11, or the way the generation before us talks about the day Kennedy was shot. For all of those events the day started as a normal day and then news came, and our emotional responses and experiences left lasting imprints in our brain, so conjuring up the memory is as vivid as if it were occurring in the present.

The exam room of Dr. Thompson's office was relatively small. There was an exam table where Sarah was sitting, smiling as usual, and talking about school. I sat in the chair next to the x-ray screen with my youngest daughter, Katelyn, who was two years old, on my lap sipping a juice box. We couldn't get in to see Dr. Thompson for months, so I settled for a colleague of his—a Dr. somebody, but I assumed that was OK. After all this was just an appointment to put my mind at ease.

As the doctor came back into the room after completing his exam and waiting to review the hip x-ray Sarah had completed an hour prior, he assured me that he saw nothing wrong with her feet, although he did notice that her arches were a bit high (ignore the sweat, ignore the knot...ignore). The hip x-ray was just to be thorough. I had talked my husband out of coming to the appointment with me because I was sure that all the doctors were right—this was nothing—and the appointment was just to ease my mind, or more specifically unravel the knot in my stomach. Now as we were waiting, I wished I had agreed to him joining us.

My attention turned back to the X-ray machine that was being turned on, and it was illuminating Sarah's hip. Hip dysplagia was being explained. Apparently, at birth Sarah's hipbone moved out of the socket, and for the next five years continued to rub and erode the socket as she walked or tried to run to first base. He went on to casually explain that they would need to surgically remove bone from her pelvis to create a new socket. They would need to cut her femur and turn it back into the joint for better alignment and she would need to be in a body cast for four months from the neck down. In total four surgeries would be required with pin placement and removal and…

The room began to spin, and simply sharing this story now, I feel physically anxious just recalling the look on Sarah's face and then her voice. "Mommy, what is he saying? Is he going to cut me? Please don't let him cut my bones. It doesn't hurt that bad when I run in gym. I want to go home." Katelyn began to cry, probably sensing the panic in the room. I have never fainted in my life, but I thought this could be the time. Everything felt dark and my mouth was so dry, I couldn't speak. My thoughts were racing. What is this insensitive, heartless, hideous man saying? He is telling me this in front of Sarah and delivering the message as if he were asking me if I wanted a cup of coffee.

I had to get out of that room. I am not sure if I said good-bye, looked at him, or how I got to my car. I remember asking to take the x-ray, helping Sarah off the table, and carrying Katie through the lobby of the medical building. I then got in my car and did what a mature grown woman would do. I went to my mother's house, put a movie on for the girls, then went to the basement with my mother and cried for hours. Jay left work early and rushed to my mother's house to be with me as I sat on the floor in the basement and sobbed in my mom's arms.

What if I could turn back the clock and pretend I didn't notice how she struggled to run to first base? Damn softball, kickball, sports…Maybe the hip wasn't perfect but not bad enough to put her through all of what was explained. I could not let that hideous man, doctor, person go near Sarah. Over the next several weeks Jay and I took Sarah and her x-ray to four different doctors in the greater Cleveland and Akron area. The four doctors were skill-fully chosen after days of reviewing their surgical reputations, bedside manner with children, seeking covert information from surgical friends of mine, and obtaining background information on their sleep and substance abuse histories. I simply wanted a surgeon who was awake, alert, drug-free, kind, and surgically the absolute best.

Ironically, that path led us back to Dr. Thompson—the real guy, not his colleague. He went on to perform four surgeries on Sarah. He was able to do it without a body cast, and she was able to return to first grade in a wheelchair for the remaining five months of school. She took the surgeries, the pain, and the inconvenience in stride. She rarely complained, always looked at the positive side of what was happening. She loved Dr. Thompson and looked forward to her office appointments with him and did her rehab mostly to please him. The one thing she did complain about was that she had to miss gym class. That made me smile.

Smiling and cheering from the front row of the bleachers, near first base, my parents, my grandmother and I watched Sarah strike out the last batter to end the inning and win the series. Sarah's father was the guy sitting on the baseball bucket calling the pitches, wearing his coach's shirt and a smile from ear to ear. Oh yeah, that's him, the guy with chest puffed way out and the tear that nobody else could see. In high school, Sarah was the pitcher on a girls' fast-pitch travel team. I loved watching her play softball. I loved watching the strength in her legs when she pushed off the mound to release a pitch, which meant the hip was fine. I loved secretly knowing that Sarah had to be a strong hitter to have a chance to make it to first base, because she still was not a fast runner. I loved seeing the look on my grandmother's face watching the sport she loves and cheering for her great-granddaughter. Nana would yell and cheer and sometimes offer Sarah advice on her curveball. After one particular game, the coach for the other team approached Sarah and told her he was inspired by the fact that her grandmother would come to so many games and cheer the way she did. Sarah corrected him and told him, "That's my great-grandmother. She is ninety-seven years old. My grandmother is the lady sitting to her right."

When Katelyn turned three years old, my grandmother bought her a plastic bat and ball and would play catch in the yard with her to get her ready for her first game. She was starting T-ball. Katelyn has always been naturally a bit more athletic like her father. On her first day, the coaches (her dad) lined her up to the T-ball stand, and slowly Katie would inch her way to the other side to hit as a lefty. She could crush that ball and soon was able to hit without the T-stand. She is right-handed but plays golf and bats as a lefty, just like her father.

Katie definitely has her dad's athletic genes. Did I mention that her father is a talented athlete? Can you believe the guy who was a gifted football player in high school and college, who is a great golfer (even when he only plays once a year, maybe), has bowled a perfect game, is a great softball player, and an incredibly knowledgeable and generous girls softball coach, that man married the girl who could not kick the ball in gym? It should be noted that he hates when I say this, because yes, as the years have gone by, I have found that I can sink the basketball when playing in the driveway, I can hit the ball when playing softball for fun, and in fact I started playing golf at the age of forty-eight and am not that bad. Granted, though, it is not kickball.

I recently read a quote from Pete Rose as he described baseball. He said, "Baseball is a team game, but nine men who reach their individual goals make a nice team." When I read this, I thought that seemed a rather odd way to describe a game that requires individuals to often sacrifice their own stats for the team. What about the power hitters who bunt to score a run instead of worrying about their own stats, and fielders who make the catch to allow the pitcher to pitch a no-hitter? That doesn't sound like individual goals to me, but maybe that was how he approached the game.

But I'm proud to say that my girls didn't approach the game that way. When I watched them play softball through the years, I always felt I learned new things about their character. How could girls who could whine and complain when they were hungry or hot be the same girls who would battle through summer heat, bruises, and cuts but would not willingly leave a game? They pushed themselves. They competed.

Off the field they could be normal, self-centered, teenage girls, but on the field they were team players. No matter how they may have wanted to swing for the fences, they would lay down the bunt as instructed to advance another teammate on the bases. They encouraged and supported each other when somebody made a bad play. They learned to use their strengths to overcome their weaknesses. Sarah pitched and used her upper-body strength to contribute to the team, while Katie and her thin stature used her great hand-eye coordination to be a surprisingly strong hitter. They learned about commitment and the importance of having a positive attitude. There was no pouting or crying in baseball. They saved that for when they got home.

Before many games, Nana would remind them to have fun and enjoy playing the game, to take in and remember how they feel when they are on that field. She wanted them to remember the feeling of winning and sharing that with their teammates, to recall the smell of their mitts and the feel of making contact with the ball with their bat. She talks about the smell of the popcorn, the sound of the bat, and the excitement of a player stealing a base. She truly absorbs and enjoys all aspects of baseball. She soaks up the game the way she absorbs moments in her life.

The metaphor of baseball and the actual game of baseball have been woven into the fabric of our family and passed on through the generations. My grandparents loved Indians baseball. They were committed fans who lived in Pennsylvania but drove to Cleveland to watch games. In fact, they were at the World Series in 1948 when the Indians won the championship.

On summer evenings they would take their places on their small screened-in front porch in their home in Akron. My grandfather would sit in his oversized, overstuffed chair that was covered in a multi-colored old quilt. He would put the old white Motorola radio on the windowsill to get the best reception and next to it he would place a Mason canning jar filled with cold coffee, lots of milk, and at least six tablets of saccharine. He would put his cane between his legs to create a stool to prop his crooked leg.

My grandmother would take her place on the yellow and white chaise lounge that was covered with a lime-green blanket and a pillow my Aunt Josephine had made that had an embroidered yellow canary on it. Nana always had a paper towel, a small Tupperware container, a metal paring knife, and some kind of fruit. She would ever so gently cut pieces of the fruit and eat them straight off the knife until literally there would only be seeds or a small core left to put in the bowl. I loved watching her eat fruit. She still cuts it the same as if she is surgically manipulating each piece with such gentle care. This would go on for hours as the game played on. The announcer's voice would get loud and describe the incredible play or the bad call, but the porch would remain silent — neither one of my grandparents spoke for fear of missing any piece of information that was being conveyed.

In stark contrast in my house today, my husband and my girls yell out, jump up from their seats, and all the while provide commentary on the plays and on the commentators. Grandma seems amused by all the antics. She laughs and agrees with everything they say. I don't know how my grandfather would have taken this behavior. I suspect he may have quietly taken his radio and went off to his garden in the backyard with his Mason jar of coffee to listen in peace. What I do know is that my grandfather would have been thrilled to know how my grandmother celebrated her birthday with the Cleveland Indians.

The sun came up on May 24, 2012, and remained out for what would be an incredible baseball celebration of Nana's one hundredth birthday. I swear Nana jumped out of bed and ran down the spiral staircase with anticipation of the day. Well, actually, it was a one-hundred-year-old kind of jump; she slid out of bed, grabbed her walker, and took off with more speed and energy than usual. This was the day. The day the oldest and biggest Indians baseball fan would celebrate her birthday with her Indians in the owner's suite. She put on her blue stretch pants that I had hemmed for her the week prior. She gently took her white jersey off the hanger and put it on, then stepped back to admire it in the mirror. The personal birthday note written on the front read, "Emily, Happy 100th Birthday. I am catching up to you. Love, Omar Vizquel #13."

Omar was one of her favorite players when he was here in Cleveland. When a reporter asked her why he was her favorite, she responded, "I loved watching him play the game. He played like he was simply playing with friends in his backyard. Always smiling and enjoying the game. That's what baseball should be all about."

When we arrived at Progressive Field, we were all escorted to the owner's suite, where Nana was surrounded by reporters from all three of the primary networks, with their cameras and lights. She sat and answered questions about what it was like to be at the World Series game when the Indians won in 1948, her favorite plays of the game, and what she loved most about baseball. She held court, answering all the questions looking into the cameras as if she had been doing this her whole life. As she was wrapping up the final interview, Curtis from the Indians hospitality group announced it was time. Nana's four generations all dressed in matching blue Indians shirts left the owner's suite to head to the elevator and then to the field.

Nana, Jay, and I exited the suite and were escorted through a tunnel on our way toward the field. The tunnel was somewhat dark with concrete floors and dull cinder blocks, but from the look on Nana's face, you would have thought we were gliding on the red carpet, awaiting our entrance into the Academy Awards. As we rounded the final corner, we were met by a golf cart carrying four of the Indians' pitchers on their way to the bullpen. They stopped to wish Nana a happy birthday and thanked her for being such an incredible fan. The dark tunnel gave way to the streaming sunshine and the noise of the crowd. We entered the playing field from left center field. The crowd greeted her with cheers and applause and many yelled happy birthday wishes to Nana.

Once we were on the field, each of the camera crews from the major networks handed me their wireless microphones to clip on the top of Nana's pants. I hooked all four of them on her and ran the microphone cords up through her shirt and clipped them on her lapel. They were heavy and seemed to be weighing down her blue stretch pants. It was almost time. Jay and I helped Nana up from her wheelchair.

As we stood there waiting, she leaned over to me, probably forgetting the microphones were on, and said, "Do these microphones make one side of my ass look bigger than the other?" I desperately tried to hold back the belly laugh as the announcer in the stadium said, "Celebrating her one-hundredth birthday is Emily Serian, who will be throwing out the first pitch."

And with that Jay and I escorted Nana toward the mound with her crooked ass and all. Standing on the pitching mound was Nana's four-year-old great-great-grandson, Xzavier. Next in line was her great-granddaughter, Alexandra, followed by her granddaughter, Diane, and finally her daughter, my mother, Joanne. The ball was handed to Xzavier, who tossed it down the line to the representative of each of the generations.

My mother then tossed it to Nana, who turned around, took a windup, and then threw an overhand pitch about twenty feet right over the plate. She admittedly did practice the week prior in the front yard with Jay. She was determined not to look like an old lady throwing a little underhanded feeble toss. The crowd cheered. The seventy-five family members in the crowd held banners with her picture on it and yelled her name. Mission accomplished.

With the biggest smile I have seen on her face in a long time, we began our journey back to the tunnel. We were almost there when they began to play the national anthem and we had to stop. As if there were divine intervention, we stopped right in front of the players as they were lined up on the third base line for the anthem. We knew that protocol was not to approach the players just before the game, but we had no idea they would approach her. As the anthem ended, the right fielder of the Cleveland Indians, Shin-Soo Choo, came over to her, bent down over the wheelchair, complimented her on her throw, and wished her a happy birthday. She thanked him and then without hesitation shook her finger at him and instructed him to hit one for her. He smiled and nodded and then ran off.

We exited the field and headed for the press room, where we would have our five-generation picture taken. We got settled in for the photo, and then news came quickly into the room that Choo, first at bat in the first inning, had just hit a homerun. Wow. Word of Nana and Choo's interaction and the result quickly spread. When we returned to the owner's suite to watch the game, owners Larry and Eva Dolan were there to wish her a happy birthday and give her a signed baseball and a cake that Slider the mascot brought in. They had a quartet sing to her, and then Larry asked her to go down to the locker room and threaten all of his players to hit homeruns. Baseball — what a game.

11 | Aging: When the Inside Doesn't Match the Outside

"I am greedy for life."

— EMILY SERIAN

A ging is a complex process. Biologists talk about aging in terms of biological decrements and overall decline in functional capacity; scientists see it as a reflection of expected changes occurring as organisms advance through the life cycle; and gerontologists talk about aging in terms of biological, psychological, and cognitive changes. There is even a description of aging as a mellowing process similar to that of the enzymatic changes associated with aging wine. What? Clearly my aging family never got the memo that we were to mellow in our senior years.

I think we all get it—well, most of us get it that as we age, our appearance changes. We develop wrinkles and gray hair everywhere (yuck), our skin sags and hangs on our bones, our ass droops, our stomach plumps out, and the ability to do jumping jacks changes. OK, well, maybe that is unique to me—what happened to my timing and coordination skills? Oh yeah, I left them in gym class years ago.

Aging introduces us to words like hemorrhoids, hypertension, gout, and incontinence. Why do we pee just a little when we sneeze or laugh? Haven't we been sneezing and laughing our whole life? Shouldn't those muscles be strong enough by now to hold back that urine? We walk slower. We are more cautious not to fall, for fear of breaking our now-fragile bones. Reading a menu in the restaurant now requires pulling out your purse and digging to the bottom to find those damn glasses that bring the items into focus but simultaneously blur the appearance of the person you are dining with— you can't win. My trick is to memorize the menu before I arrive at the restaurant or simply to make up my own unique dish. That way I appear sophisticated and in control as opposed to old and blind. I think Aunt Joan would have appreciated this maneuver.

These beautiful outward changes that occur with aging never seem to line up with how we feel on the inside. We think we are young and capable beyond what our bodies say. This disconnection between how we look on the outside and how we feel on the inside seems universal. I rarely hear somebody say that he feels so old on the inside but looks vibrant on the outside—unless he is delusional. No, most people will say, "I still feel thirty" when they are in their forties; or in my case at fifty, I feel—not sure yet, as I am still trying to figure out what my choices are. But in Nana's case, she reports that at one hundred, she still feels eighty. It was a good decade for her.

I always thought that Gram never acted her age. That is not to say that she was immature. It is that she was always adventurous and open-minded for her age. As a child, I knew she was old. I mean, she was a grandma. But she never seemed to think like one, and she never smelled old. She smelled like great face lotions. Maybe she was never told that old people were to have traditional values, be conservative, and grow in maturity, aka seriousness. I don't think she ever got that memo either. I always enjoyed spending time with her. I never really saw her physically or emotionally as old—just as my grandmother. Aging has not changed that for her. I know her outside has morphed into a more wrinkled bent person, but inside her spirit is the same. She continues to be that funny, kind-hearted woman who can make you feel special and valued, no matter what your age or hers.

As the car stopped in the parking space, I stretched to see over the windshield. We were here. I reached for my little pink leather purse. I put it over my shoulder, holding tight to it when I closed the car door as if it held valuable objects. In reality, the contents included a zippered change case, some gum, and a hairbrush, but carrying that purse was an important part of the routine. I felt so grown up.

She got out of the car and reached down for my hand; we walked through the parking lot and into the store. As always, we were hit by the smell of popcorn that had recently been popped and the sight of French fries cooking in the fryer. The counter bar top was stark white, which provided great contrast for the plastic red ketchup and bright yellow mustard bottles that sat in the center. The bar stools were round and covered in red leather, with a bright shiny chrome base that swiveled. From every stool there was the view of the mirrored back wall, which reflected the mint-green milkshake machine and the chrome containers that were filled with ice cream. In the corner stood the glass case, which displayed the green bottles of Coca-Cola. The semi- circle counter encircled the waitress who was smiling, wearing her usual pale-blue uniform dress, her white shoes, and the tight hair bun that made her face look plastic.

I knew we would have our snack at the counter but only after we made our purchases. I loved the shopping process, but I especially loved sitting on those red stools next to her. It made me feel special and grown-up. Shopping in Woolworths with Grandma was always an adventure. We started in one aisle and would methodically make our way up and down each one, examining every one of the different items. We could spend hours examining the merchandise. It always seemed striking to me that she never appeared to be in a hurry. Hurry up was never uttered, nor did our pace seem quick or rushed. On the contrary, the time spent in each aisle was slow and deliberate, like we were enjoying a delicious treat we didn't want to waste. We were savoring our time in Woolworths with each other. Perhaps that is why the memory remains so vivid. The details were catalogued.

On this particular day, we shopped the aisles, but we were on a mission: I was going to get my first bottle of nail polish.

Grandma treated this purchase as if it held the same importance as selecting the right attire for a bride on her wedding. It was my first and I had no idea what color to choose. We stood before the rows and rows of polish. Carefully and methodically she would lift one from the shelf and ask what I thought of this pink one or this red one. No, they weren't what I was looking for. And then my eye caught the pale blue bottle labeled "Skyblue." It was beautiful. I don't think I had ever seen that color on anybody's fingers before.

She smiled at me and said, "That is quite a color. I wonder what Gramps will say." What indeed. We both knew that in his old-fashioned style, he would oppose all nail polish for a girl my age or a woman at any age, for that matter. He would most certainly have strong feelings about *blue* polish. I felt a quick feeling of worry rise up. Maybe this was not a good color; I wondered if Grandpa would yell at her if she bought it for me. I thought for a while and then slowly put it back on the shelf.

Gram looked at me and smiled. "I think this is a beautiful blue, and I like this canary yellow one as well. Let's get them both." She gently put them into our basket and took them to the register to pay. She did it again. With one sentence, she washed away all doubt or insecurity. I felt important and confident. Confident but not stupid, we both agreed not to show Gramps the nail polish when we got home or — ever. He wouldn't understand the things women buy on their shopping trips. Like the time Gram bought me a red stir-fry wok.

The wok seemed to be screaming from the shelf for our attention. Neither one of us had ever used one before, but without hesitation she bought it for me. She was adventurous — not like what I knew of my friend's grandmothers, who may have thought this to be an odd purchase. But not her; she tried new things all the time. It was easy to be swept up in her enthusiasm for trying things — for buying new kitchen gadgets, or oh yeah, face cream. At the age of seventy-five years old, she forgot about the important message that you are to mellow and knit when you age.

We put the wok in the car and I committed to making dinner for her and me and Gramps that evening. I sliced vegetables and chicken and cooked it all per the directions. The onions, peppers, and zucchini made the kitchen smell incredible. When I added them to the chicken, they created a festive-looking bowl in that red wok. I gently placed the wok with all of its contents into the center of the table. She and I looked at each other. What a work of art. How cool were we, cooking in a wok.

We called Gramps to eat. He took a look at the wok, and his words were, "What the hell is that?" *I heard*, "That looks interesting, what is that?" His bark was always worse than his sentiments. He got a different memo. The one that says, "One should get grouchy as you get older and never, never try new things." No harm. I began to explain that it was a stir-fry. Try it. "For Christ sake, the vegetables are raw." he barked. Gram piped in, "Nope, they are al dente. Just like the recipes say they should be. You are an old fart." Then she laughed but proceeded to take his dish to the microwave to turn the vegetables into "mush" — just the way he liked them. He ate and she and I laughed that night and many other nights whenever I pulled the wok out to make dinner. We felt proud of our creative adventurous selves.

In reviewing Nana's life and dividing it in half, it has become very clear that her first fifty years were filled with much physical illness and emotional and financial struggles. She looked so old and sick in many of the pictures before she turned fifty. Her past fifty years have been the kick-ass years. She has gone on more family vacations, learned new cooking techniques, and maintained her sense of humor and her adventurous spirit. She has been in her best physical health — that's probably because during her first fifty years, the doctors removed almost every organ she had, leaving nothing to be plagued by disease. Her remaining organs include a quarter of her stomach, several feet of intestines, and an incredible heart.

As I approach fifty, I am working on finding the courage to look around the bend of my life's path. Am I at the halfway point? Am I three quarters of the way there or less? I am finding that it is true when people talk about every decade of life bringing something new. I received a doctoral degree in my twenties, had babies in my thirties, really found my confidence, my voice, and my rhythm in my forties. Well, not actual rhythm; some things we don't grow into or develop with age. It is my rhythm of life — my passion and purpose have become clearer.

I fear leaving my forties because they have been so great. It was the decade that I almost lost my Jay to a pulmonary embolism, almost lost my grandmother to a bowel obstruction, and almost lost my dad to renal cancer. But I didn't. It was the decade I saw Sarah and Katie enter high school, start to drive, hold their first jobs…I saw Sarah graduate from high school, go off to college, and vote for the first time for the president of the United States. I saw my beautiful nieces get married. I held and played with my incredible great-nephews. I watched my grandmother turn one hundred years old, throw out the first pitch at a Major League game, and held her as she lay over the casket of her son. It is so strange to reflect on life this way with both an appreciation for so much and yet always mixed in with the sadness and loss that comes with living.

There are only a few things that I do know about my fifties. I know my children will be grown, probably out of college and out of the house. Maybe the next ten years will usher in weddings for my girls and possibly grandbabies. That fills me with pride and excitement. If I look at probabilities and statistics, this will probably be the decade I will lose my grandmother. And those are only the things that I *can* anticipate. I know there will be a mixture of incredible blessings and deep sorrows that await me over the next decade that are unknown to me.

My birthday wish for myself is that despite the fear of looking ahead and anticipating what is to come as a fifty-year-old woman, that I hold tight to Nana's voice. That I remain greedy for life. I wish that I live each day truly knowing that the moment I am standing in is all I know for sure. I want to greet each moment knowing this could be that moment that makes it to my next memoir — the one that stands out as an extraordinary gift, which I will savor and tuck away to be used later when painful losses and disappointments wash over me.

I wish that I would always feel younger on the inside then I look on the outside. And I wish that I would always look younger on the outside than my birth certificate says I am. I'm just saying...

I hope I keep Nana's spirit of integrity and her gift of forgiving. That I always, always remember how to laugh and I maintain a sense of adventure and joy in living, even when things get hard. And above all I pray that I never lose her voice. That raspy, rough, screechy voice guides me when I am lost, points me in the direction of doing good, that I remember to swallow my pride and forgive because it will make me feel better, and that I remember that a life without gratitude is an empty one.

My birthday gift to me will be to continue to make Nana proud by pursuing my purpose here on earth with all the passion and commitment it deserves.

12 Celebrating 100 Years of Life with Gratitude

"I expect to pass through life but once. If therefore, there be any kindness I can show, or any good thing I can do to any fellow being, let me do it now, and not defer or neglect it, as I shall not pass this way again."

— WILLIAM PENN

The alarm went off at 6:00 a.m. Well, not the kind that has numbers and a beeping sound. The one that somehow set up camp in my head about ten years ago, which made the need for an actual clock and the chance to sleep late obsolete. But on this day there was no desire to sleep in; the excitement of the day made the household jump out of bed as if we had all had several shots of espresso. It was Nana's one-hundredth birthday party, and soon 260 family and friends from across the country would be arriving at our house to celebrate.

The house was already filled with the kind of family noises, smells, and energy that made me smile. Jay had the coffee brewing. My great-nephews were running in their jammies through the house, eating cookies and driving their cars across the kitchen floor. Jennifer was trying to sit on the bar stool at the counter, but her big pregnant belly was keeping her a good foot and half from her coffee cup. My nephews, Trevor and Doug, were already outside setting up all 260 chairs under the massive tent and were making sure that the two Porta-Potties lining the driveway were working. My niece, Stephanie, the party planner, was downstairs with her clipboard and coffee, gently barking out orders. Yes, despite what our husbands may say, we Stevic woman are gentle about how we give orders. Well, everybody but my sister Diane, whose bark makes us all jump. She was in the kitchen giving instructions to her husband on how the fruit should be cut up.

I stepped outside as the sun was just coming up in the eastern sky, with orange and purple colors being cast across the pool. The planning of this party began six months prior, with all the worries that go with party planning and the need for alternate plans in the event of rain, cold temperatures, humidity, or extreme heat. But on this May 26, 2012, the day was to be perfect.

The tent was erected four days prior by fifteen men in hard hats. When I rented the tent, I was told it was 3,200 square feet and could accommodate our 260 guests, plus a stage, lights, and ceiling fans, but somehow I never envisioned an entire structure being put up in my yard. Metal beam ceilings, side walls with windows, and expanding canvas created an image of a large white home. Inside, the pink, lime, orange, lavender, and yellow sherbet-colored tables with the centerpieces of old-fashioned Coke bottles filled with red roses and iris flowers created a festive scene.

Tables were lined along the base of the swimming pool, set with rows of silver chafing dishes where the main course would be served. During the planning phases, we all agreed that while we have a family tradition of cooking, and eating for that matter, we would cater a party for 260 people. However, as time got closer, my mother was heard saying, "Well, I am just going to make a few stuffed cabbages and maybe some homemade stuffed manicotti." So, after making 350 stuffed cabbages, 320 homemade cheese-filled manicotti and pasta, Mom finally agreed to have the salad catered. What a load off our minds.

My mother also made a three-tiered white cake that was adorned with pastel-colored flowers and one hundred candles. In addition, my father spent the better part of three months re-creating the Cleveland Indians stadium. He tiled and grouted the entrance way to the field where the Bob Feller statue sits, including exact replicas of the advertising banners, lights, grass, and the infield. He even filled the stands with clay-made baseball fans wearing baseball hats. On the outside path sat another cake made in the shape of a baseball diamond with Nana's picture in her Indians jersey rotating at the top. There were four other flavored cakes, cheesecakes, an ice-cream cart, and of course a popcorn machine. The designer popcorn buckets had a photo of Nana with her saying of the day: "Eat popcorn every day. It helps with digestion and makes you feel like you are watching baseball."

Displayed for the guests was also a replica of Nana's tickets from the 1948 World Series when the Cleveland Indians won, the jersey she wore when she threw out the first pitch just days prior, and photos of her with the owners of the Cleveland Indians. But my eye caught the Motorola radio on which she and Grandps listened to the game for so many years. As the sun moved higher on the horizon, it felt like maybe he would be with us for the day.

The day was in fact weather perfect, the food was incredible, desserts decadent, music soothing (oh yeah, there was a band), but nothing was more perfect than the moment Nana took the stage. She was dressed in a beautiful blue blouse that made her Polish blue eyes shine. She took the microphone and greeted her guests, which included family from seven different states, with three, sometimes four, generations represented. Her two remaining siblings sat in the front row.

"I want to thank everyone for being here to celebrate my life," she said. "I am so happy that we are gathered together as a family today while my eyes are still open to see all of you…and to enjoy the party."

The photographer snapped a photo of her smiling. She was beaming with joy from a deep place. What a stark contrast to the photos of her on her ninetieth birthday. I remember that day.

We celebrated her ninetieth birthday at my parent's home during a beautiful weekend in May 2002. Friends and family came to celebrate with her. The white tents were set up in the driveway, and table after table of food was set up in the basement. Nana wore a striking teal sweater set with white slacks and a white corsage pinned to her sweater, but her face wore no real smile.

In almost every picture from her ninetieth birthday, she is smiling, but it looks plastic as if it took great effort. It was the kind of smile you make when you know it is expected but it doesn't come from a place of real happiness. The muscles around her mouth were tense and her eyes seemed empty. She seemed so sad and so lost. I began to recall the conversation I had with her the day before her ninetieth birthday party.

My mother was cooking and my sisters were both working on the final touches for the display tables. I curled up on the couch with Nana and asked her what was bothering her. Per usual in our family, the answer was nothing, nothing, nothing, and then oh yeah, maybe there was something bothering her.

She took a deep breath and said, "I was thinking about what is next for me." Next? What did she mean by next? She started to talk about feeling nervous and scared. This of course made her feel physically ill and more frail and fragile than she really was. She started to click her fingernails together, which usually means she is stressed and worried. It was clear turning ninety was the first real turning point for her, the first time she was struck by her own mortality. I asked the question that perhaps was the obvious one, but one I hoped would not scare her more. I asked her if she was afraid to die.

She thought for a long while and then said, "I don't want to say good-bye. I don't want to leave my family." It took ninety years and so many illnesses and near-death experiences for her to face her own mortality. And she was scared. I was lying with my head on her shoulder, and she gently pushed me up and looked me in the eye and asked me if I would do her a favor. I mouthed, "Of course," but deep inside felt a sense of fear creeping into my stomach.

"Would you be willing to do my eulogy at my funeral?" she asked. I wanted to laugh. I wanted to slap her in some silly way. I wanted to say, "Are you crazy, old lady?" But I responded, "I would be honored." At that moment when I smiled and agreed and I saw the relief on her face, I felt it again, the depth of how much she loves me. I would not let her down, no matter how hard that speech would be. We put this topic to bed for the night as we had a birthday to celebrate in the morning. But in remembering the pictures from her ninetieth celebration, maybe the topic, the nerves, and the physical distress that often accompanied her worry was not really put away.

I spent the next several months thinking about her eulogy. I wondered how you honor and say good-bye to…to her. I felt a sense of urgency to complete it. I wanted to be prepared, to be ready. I wrote about the human being that she is, the life lessons she has given, and her great contributions to this world. I cried and laughed all the while I was putting my thoughts and memories to paper. When it was finished, I printed it on linen paper and filed it in a drawer under "Nana."

Shortly after her ninety-first birthday, we were chatting on the couch, eating popcorn, and I told her I had written her eulogy. I laughed. "I wrote it a year ago thinking you could die at any time and I wanted to be ready." I told her how hard and meaningful it was for me to write it. I went to the drawer and took it out of the folder. I wanted her to hear it. So I read it to her. She cried, I cried, and then she spoke with that devilish twinkle in her eye and the smirk around her mouth.

"That's beautiful. There better not be a dry eye in the crowd. I want everybody to be crying, no, I want them to be sobbing because they miss me so much. And I don't want people chatting, laughing, and "packing" (a strange family word for overeating) themselves with food. If I can't be there enjoying the party, then they all should be miserable. You should add that to the eulogy." Now I am not sure I can deliver the eulogy without laughing and recalling her words.

Periodically we laugh about her sentiments on the eulogy and her hopes for the dismal and sad funeral. As a matter of fact, she did remind me the other day that the eulogy is now ten years old and probably should be updated. "I know I have done and said some interesting things worth talking about over the past ten years," she said. She is right again.

My grandmother has lived a very long life. Over the course of her one hundred years, she knew the love and sacrifice of her poor parents. She learned to appreciate nature, hard work, and independence from working the family farm as a child. She knew the struggles of being raised in a large family of seventeen children when there was barely enough money for food and clothes. She knew what it was like to go to school and be made fun of and ridiculed for how she dressed. She experienced the unbearable pain of losing her first baby at the age of ten months to pneumonia and then many decades later, buried her son at the age of seventy from cancer. She has been without my grandfather for the past twenty-seven years. She has buried her parents and fourteen of her brothers and sisters. And through it all she consistently finds gratitude in all of her joyful and painful memories.

There were so many decisions and choices to make over the course of her life, each one leading to disappointments, failures, opportunities, and incredible joy and success. As she spoke further from that stage about her life, I was so keenly aware how her life was now being proportionately reviewed more than experienced. I started to wonder what her life might look like today, if one decision or event would have been different. Ironically, *she* never thinks like that; her stories and memories focus on how much she appreciates the little things. She holds on to moments of every positive and happy life experience, savoring them so she can occasionally pull them out of her memory and reexperience them again.

There is no arguing that this life is short, temporary, and yet so filled with opportunities to fulfill our purpose. We rely on the voices in our head to guide us in our choices and decisions when we reach a divide on our path. I have learned to rely on gratitude for all that seems small and insignificant, as I understand that these are the sentiments that carry us when the disappointments and painful moments come for all of us. Those heavy moments that stay with us.

For me, there is that moment when the coroner wheeled my grandfather out of his house for the last time after his long battle with cancer ended. We moved the dining room table for the gurney to pass—the same table that for so many years we shared great food, laughter, and so much love. The table he had walked around and around in a futile attempt to regain the strength that the cancer was daily taking from him. The moment hardly seemed real as they took him through the living room and out the front door. As I stared at the wheel marks that the gurney made across the living room carpet, I had images of the gifts Santa had left on that same floor and the Easter baskets filled with candy that my grandfather would make and hide in that living room, on that carpet.

There was the moment when the brief phone call from the mother of a twenty-three-year-old patient of mine. The empty-sounding pain-struck voice vibrated through the phone. She told me that Joe had successfully committed suicide the night before. I never forgot her voice or the reality of what I do for a living.

There was the painful moment when I first saw my mother's face at the funeral of her brother. She seemed so fragile and broken. I had a flash of insight that one day I may be standing at the funeral of my sisters or them at mine.

Through my painful moments and disappointments, I remember Grandma's words. "We are all here for a purpose," she says. As I watched her on the stage sharing her stories, it became clear to me that these were not just words she used or a nice saying for an inspirational calendar. She lived it—she *was* living it. I don't pretend to know what she believes her purpose is, but I know that for me her purpose on this earth has been to guide me to mine. Her voice pushes me forward with passion to be grateful for all the moments that were painful but brought me incredible gifts, and to appreciate fully the incredible moments that in real time may have only lasted for minutes, even though the joyful feeling they create lasts forever and a day. Nana is right. It is those short joyful moments that carry us through life.

As I approach the celebration of my fifty years of life, I have begun to reminisce on those fleeting moments that have passed, but when conjured up in my memory, remind me how grateful I am for this life. Two little pieces of video sit on the desktop of my computer. One is a clip of my daughter Sarah when she was two-and-a-half years old. She is wearing a Tupperware bowl on her head, talking on her little phone while my husband is filming her. She looks into the camera and tells him her name, 'I'm Sarah Emily Rust." She tells him she is talking on the phone to a policeman. She states, "He is a nice person." She dances and smiles with that bowl on her head and goes on to tell him, "I live in Newbury, Ohio with all my friends." Every time I watch this clip that lasts only one minute and five seconds, my heart pulls with such love and warmth.

The other video clip is of my daughter Katie at the age of two wearing her pink princess nightgown, decorating her little Christmas tree. Christmas music can be heard playing in the background, and her little tree is standing on the kitchen floor surrounded by boxes and tissue paper that she tore through to get to her special ornaments. I am holding the video camera, asking her what she is putting on her tree. "The angel, the baby, and this..." The little voice trails on, and she bounces from box to box with such enthusiasm. Her big sister is heard off camera telling her to be careful and not to shake that round box because she may break something delicate. Katie looks at her sister from the corner of her eye and then gently, ever so gently, shakes that very box and then bounces back to her tree. That little mischievous twinkle still belongs to her. I cry every time I watch this clip. It lasts one minute and twenty-one seconds.

There are other moments that I hold onto so tight for fear that time will erase them from my memory. I recall the first time I held Sarah in my arms after she was born and the first glimpse of Katie being born. I remember the look on my husband's face when he first saw me coming down the aisle in my wedding dress on my father's arm in the church on our wedding day. It was a short moment, but there would only be one first-time moment. Every Wednesday I have lunch with Jay and am still surprised at the feeling I get that first moment when I see him enter the restaurant.

There is that moment when my parents first held each of my girls after they were born. The moment the doctor said my father was cancer free. There is the moment my sisters and I smeared anniversary cake on one another's face when my parents refused to do such an impolite thing to each other on their fiftieth wedding anniversary. So, so we stepped in. I remember the taste of my mother's chicken soup that she still brings me when I am sick and the feel of the dirt when I first dig in my garden after a long winter. There is that moment when I hear the sound of my friend's voice on the phone when I have had a long day and the laugh of my nieces when I call them to share a funny story.

There are those times when Nana stays with us, and despite how she may be feeling, there is always a smile at the end of the day. Always as we tuck her into bed, she says, "Thank you for the day. I love you. I will see you for coffee." I love those moments.

From the time I was a little girl to the present day, Nana has always said, "So long" when we depart, never good-bye. "So long" always struck me as such a different way to say good-bye. My friends' grandmothers never used that term. We never used that term in our family. I recently looked up the origin of the word. It is thought to come from an Irish word "slàn," which is short for "slàn go foil," which translated means good-bye for now. For Nana the emphasis was always on the "for now" part. It was never meant to be forever in the way that good-bye implied.

It occurred to me ten years ago, she wasn't ready to say good-bye at ninety. The thought brought her great distress and anxiety. However, now, at one hundred years old, she seems to be saying, "So long" to us. Good-bye is forever and so long is temporary. She is beginning to ease us into a life here without her. She seems to be reminiscing more about her time here on earth. Her pride and satisfaction with her family make her smile. There doesn't seem to be any desperation or sadness in her voice, just more resolution and acceptance.

I admit that the concept of her not being here scares me. Intellectually, I clearly understand that the time gets closer every day. She reminds all of us that the challenge is to live knowing there is an end — reminding us to make conscious choices about what to expend energy and fear on and where to place our passions and our heart.

As my attention turned back to her on the stage, I watched her — really watched her as if time had stood still. She was talking to family, laughing and reminiscing, and in that moment I felt the power of gratitude. I absorbed that moment. I knew I would play it again and again. It is our joyful life moments that, when stacked together, give us the strength to get through the inevitable painful experiences and losses that come with life.

As Nana exited the stage, we all raised our glasses to toast. "Here is to the journey of life."

Acknowledgments

As a proud member of a five generation family, I knew that writing a memoir would not only involve sharing my own intimate stories but would involve sharing those of my family. It is with deep gratitude that I acknowledge their willingness to allow me to give my version of the story.

With every accomplishment, I have been blessed with people in front of me pulling and encouraging me along and an equal number of individuals behind me pushing and supporting me through. First and foremost, I would like to acknowledge my husband, Jay for his endless encouragement and consistent love. He makes every accomplishment feel real and every disappointment insignificant. To my beautiful daughters, Sarah and Katie who make my life stories meaningful. A special thanks to my parents for giving me the courage to find my passion and the confidence to achieve it. I am so grateful to have two amazing sisters, Diane and Leanne who simply love me. Great big hugs to my nieces, Jennifer, Stephanie, Nicole, Alexandra and Dominique — you will always be the little girls in pig tails who make me so proud. My sweetest great nephews, Xzavier, Lennox and Nixon who make me feel young. And to all of those who became my family simply by saying, "I do" especially my brothers- in-law, Jim and Skip, thank you for making my sisters so happy.

I wish to extend my deepest gratitude to my dear friend and colleague, Deborah Plummer who not only encouraged me to write this book but who provided guidance every step of the way. For the past thirty two years, she has been my teacher, my mentor and a cherished friend. To my prettiest, prettiest friends, Susan, Danialle and Becky, you consistently inspire me. Janet, Bev, Anita, Lori and Andrea, there are no words to express what your friendship and support has meant to me over the past two decades. To the many patients who have entrusted me with their life stories, your courage and strength has been an inspiration. I offer a great big thank you to my team of experts, for their editorial, graphic design and marketing support. You made the process smooth.

Finally, to my incredible grandmother, Emily, I carry you with me in my heart.

CPSIA information can be obtained at www.ICGtesting.com
Printed in the USA
LVOW121059140413

329050LV00004B/542/P